LITERARY HISTORY OF HEBREW GRAMMARIANS AND LEXICOGRAPHERS

ACCOMPANIED BY UNPUBLISHED TEXTS

By

HARTWIG HIRSCHFELD, Ph.D.

WIPF & STOCK • Eugene, Oregon

Wipf and Stock Publishers
199 W 8th Ave, Suite 3
Eugene, OR 97401

Literary History of Hebrew Grammarians and Lexicographers
Accompanied by Unpublished Texts
By Hirschfeld, Hartwig
Softcover ISBN-13: 978-1-7252-8605-4
Hardcover ISBN-13: 978-1-7252-8606-1
eBook ISBN-13: 978-1-7252-8607-8
Publication date 8/14/2020
Previously published by Oxford University Press, 1926

This edition is a scanned facsimile of the original edition published in 1926.

PREFACE

IN 1892 the late Professor W. Bacher published his treatise: *Die hebräische Sprachwissenschaft vom 10. bis zum 16. Jahrhundert,* in which he gave a full account of all that had previously been written on the matter. In the meantime enough fresh material has been unearthed to justify a resumption of the work, adding new points of view, while laying stress on the pragmatic development of linguistic studies.

Since this essay has been sent to the press, an article by the late Dr. S. Poznański: 'New material on the history of Hebrew-Arabic philology during the X–XII centuries' (*JQR.*, N. S., xvi, pp. 237 seqq.) has appeared, dealing chiefly with Professor Kokovzov's discoveries. These have all been discussed in the following pages. Dr. Poznański has left unmentioned several important names which should not have been omitted.

H. H.

TABLE OF CONTENTS

INTRODUCTION

As long as Hebrew was a living language there was apparently neither necessity nor occasion for analytical treatment. On the other hand the Bible itself furnishes instances of rudimentary trials at linguistic explanation connected with several primitive words, and especially proper names such as חוה, אשה, יוסף, משה, מנשה, אפרים, and others. This, of course, does not mean any systematic endeavour to expound roots, or the grammatical value of forms. Only when the post-biblical reader was faced with the task of studying the holy text for legal, liturgical, or educational purposes was he forced to look more closely into the formation of words as well as the structure of sentences. Portions of the Law, Prophets, and Hagiographa had to be recited correctly, and, if occasion demanded, translated for the benefit of the people. The persons appointed to discharge this duty had to make themselves acquainted with the Hebrew and Aramaic vocabularies in their various grammatical aspects. We may, therefore, assume that the *Methurgemān*, or public translator of the Pentateuch into the Aramaic vernacular (*Targum*), was in the main responsible for the earliest attempts at a scientific treatment of the Hebrew language. As many portions of these translations are merely paraphrastic, this kind of work cannot be called grammatical research. At the same time necessity was felt to fix the reading of the text in respect of correct spelling, and to establish rules for the use of copyists and readers. These rules formed part of the *Halākhāh*, and were comprised under the name of *Māsōrah*, which was the work of Palestinian authorities. An important step towards regular linguistic studies was made by the introduction of the two systems of vowel signs and diacritical points,[1] which did not take place till the sixth or seventh century. The beginning of this work was probably of still earlier date, since the Babylonian Amorā R. Āshē (about 400) is credited with the authorship of a *Sēpher Hanniqqūd* (*Book of Punctuation*). The Talmud tractate *Sōpherim*, composed about 600 in Palestine, which in twenty-one chapters contains the rules for the writing of the scrolls, already mentions accents, and notifies several differences between the traditions of eastern and western Jews. In course of time the Māsōrah was separated from the Halākhāh, and devoted to the task of fixing the rules of vocalization and accentuation. The origin of the Hebrew vowel-signs is still somewhat problematic, although various theories have been advanced for their elucidation. It is a strange phenomenon that the Hebrew square alphabet is not a direct descendant of the ancient style of writing, but was transformed through the intermediary of the pagan Nabataeans, while the older characters passed over to the Samaritans. Nor is the use of dots a Jewish invention, but has its origin in Palmyrene inscriptions, and appears in Syro-Christian manuscripts dating from the beginning of the fifth century. The Māsōretes did not hesitate to adopt these two reforms, but took care to make cursive writing impossible by the strict prohibition of ligatures. The Māsōrah itself was subsequently enlarged by collections of variants undertaken by Ben Asher of Tiberias, and Ben Naphtali of Babylon in the tenth century. In some manuscripts the notes of both are written in columns one next to the other, but as a rule on the margins. All these endeavours served in the first instance liturgical purposes, and it is doubtful whether the Jews would have spontaneously developed synthetic grammar, had they not been urged to do so by external influences.

At the time of the Geonim, Babylon, being then under

[1] See my article, 'The Dot in Semitic Palaeography', *J.Q.R.* 1919, pp. 159 seqq.

Arab dominion, was the foremost centre of Jewish intellectual life. In the eighth and the following centuries the Arabs had created a prodigious scientific activity. Philosophy, medicine, astronomy, poetry, and other disciplines flourished. Baghdād, the capital, was the seat of famous linguists, who lectured to numerous students on the intricacies of the Arab language. It is certain that also Jews whose vernacular was Arabic were among their disciples either in person or as readers of their works.[1] There exists positive evidence that Arabic influence is visible even in the first efforts of Hebrew philology. For the Hebrew names of the three principal vowels, *a, i, u*,[2] and eve the word for *vowel*,[3] are mere translations from the Arabic. Moreover, the earliest works by Jews on the Hebrew language are not only written in Arabic, but arranged on the plan of their Arab models—adopting their terminology. There is, however, a characteristic difference between the two undertakings. While for Arab grammarians the minute elaboration of the finesses of their language became an end in itself, Jews brought their linguistic endeavours into the service of the study of the Holy Writ.

Great uncertainty prevails as to the question whether the honour of having initiated grammatical studies belongs to the Rabbanites or to the Qaraites. It is not, however, difficult to perceive that the latter were naturally more concerned in such studies than the former. For the practice of the law, which was the most important factor in Jewish life, Rabbanite Jews relied on the rabbinic tradition, whilst their actual studies on the language were more or less a luxury, reserved for the more inquisitive amongst them. Qaraites, on the other hand, based their religious life on the holy text direct, and were driven to the scrutiny of the meanings of words and sentences with meticulous care. This is not mere idle speculation, but is supported by historical evidence which shows that the earliest gramma-

[1] Ibid., 1906, Jan., Genizah extract from Sibawaihi.

[2] *fatḥa, kesra, ḍamma.*

[3] *ḥaraka*, 'movement'.

tical statement known at present belongs to the Qaraite Nissi b. Noah, who flourished in the first half of the ninth century.[1] His brief note on the use of the numeral reveals more than a bare acquaintance with the rule he expounds, and opens the view of systematic study in the background. A curious fact is that his remark does not refer to biblical Hebrew, but to a passage in the Mishnah. This is a mere coincidence as he criticizes the Mishnah which is written in Hebrew. Nissi had the correct notion that the same rules should apply as to the classical language. Another important feature speaking for the early age of this note is that it is written in Hebrew, because it is known that Jews did not employ Arabic for their writings prior to the tenth century.

Was Nissi the only Qaraite grammarian of his time? We have no means of ascertaining this, because the records are so scant and so little reliable that great caution is necessary in drawing conclusions. On the other hand, it is improbable that for the next seventy years afterwards no grammarian should have appeared in the field. Some confirmation of this is given by the famous Qaraite Solomon b. Jerōham, a younger contemporary of Sa'adyāh, who mentions 'the grammarian Abu Ya'qub Al Bakhtawi',[2] adding to his name the formula which describes him as deceased. He, therefore, must have lived before Sa'adyāh, or was an older contemporary. Of his writings nothing has been saved.

[1] The late Dr. Poznánski, see *JQR.*, N.S., xi, p. 237 seqq., contests my suggestion that the fragment in question dates from the ninth century and is in the author's autograph. All his arguments, however, are of negative character and, therefore, unconvincing. As he only saw the facsimile of a small portion of the fragment he was hardly in a position to judge its age. Besides, were it later than Sa'adyāh it would unquestionably have been written in Arabic. The discussion concerning the date of Nissi should now be considered closed. Hadāsi does not seem to have been quite straight in the matter, and Graetz's assertion that Nissi lived in the ninth century holds good. If this be the case he could not possibly have criticized Sa'adyāh, and this also affects the criticism concerning the calendar note.

[2] See Steinschneider, *ALJ.* p. 88.

The earliest attempt to arrange the letters of the Hebrew alphabet phonetically was made by the author of the Sēpher Yeṣīrāh. He distinguishes three classes: (1) Fundamental letters, א, מ, ש, which represent the first, middle, and last of the letters; (2) seven letters with twofold pronunciation, viz. בגדכפת and ר; (3) thirteen simple consonants comprising the remainder of the alphabet. The mystical element inherent in this division shows that the author of the book was not animated by grammatical considerations, but at all events he has the merit of having given an opportunity for grammatical research, as we are able to gather from the writings of the man who is justly styled the father of Hebrew grammarians.

CHAPTER I

Saʿadyāh, Qirqisāni, Judah b. Qoreish, Dūnāsh b. Tamīm, David b. Abraham.

ALTHOUGH, as we have seen, he was not actually the first Jewish grammarian, Saʿadyāh is the first Jewish author known at present who has left records of philological research. These seem to have been the firstfruits of his literary efforts stimulated by his study of Arab grammarians. This suggestion is borne out by the fact that in his first work, which he composed at the age of twenty-one years, he mentions the titles of various Arab writings dealing with elegance of style. The aim of this work was to provide a dictionary of the Hebrew language, which at the same time should assist liturgical poets in constructing acrostics and finding suitable rhymes. The work was, therefore, of duplicate appearance, being alphabetically arranged according to the initial and final letters of the words. Each item was illustrated by a quotation from the Bible or some rabbinic writing. The title of the book is *Agrōn.* Unfortunately so little of it has been preserved that we are unable to form an adequate idea of its contents. We are, however, in possession of the Hebrew introduction, which yields some interesting information. The author lays down in it some elementary principles, such as the composition of words from two parts, one fundamental, the other accessory. The latter serves the three purposes of indicating plurality, ownership, and tenses. While the fundamental part of the word remains unchanged, the accessory letters are subject to variations. These comprise the eleven consonants, א, ב, ה, ו, י, כ, ל, מ, נ, ש, ת. Four of these letters (א, י, נ, ת) are the formative letters of the imperfect tense. The introduction here ends abruptly.

Saʿadyāh seems to have been aware of some imperfectness in this work, because not long afterwards he added an Arabic translation of the words discussed, as well as an Arabic preface with the new title *Book of Poetics.* This is characteristic of the predominance of Arabic in the literary life in Moslim lands. The preface in question is fortunately extant, with the exception of the first few sentences, but is so eminently instructive, betraying the future philosopher, that it is essential to insert here a specimen in translation, although the text is uncertain in various passages.

. . . although the roots of accidences are nine while the branches are numberless. Of these I have devoted special attention to the accidence called possession [of a thing] which man calls his own. Some portions of this class are within his grasp, while others remain without.? I have to deal with the former and especially the psychical side of it, viz. knowledge. Knowledge, I say, is conditioned by the physical mutability to which a person is necessarily subjected. Whoever is possessed of knowledge should make the most of it,[1] and propagate it in order to obviate any forgetfulness which is in the wake of physical change.? The Prophets have called attention to this (however obvious it be to intelligent people) in Prov. 8. 34, which teaches that assiduity prevents forgetting. They also remind us that indolence causes forgetfulness as stated in[2] Prov. 19. 15. They compare knowledge and all it includes to the care taken of a field which is neither tilled nor sown, but bears thistles, as taught in Prov. 24. 30. Let the mindful think of Prov. 24. 32. Just as the knowledge of the individual is lost from heedlessness, so is that of a multitude forgotten for the same reason. I have seen in my life many students who asserted that much of historical and philological learning has been lost to mankind, such as the *Book of Weights*[3] and the *Book of Beginnings*,[4] &c. The Arabs also saw that some of their great men

[1] Harkawy, *StM.*, p. מ״א reads יתראדפה, but the Hebrew is לדרוש.
[2] Harkawy, ibid., ואבדנו, read ואבדָנו. [3] As yet unknown.
[4] Likewise unknown, unless he means his commentary on the Sēpher Yeṣīrāh.

observed people neglecting the purity of language; so I compiled a compendium to lead them to correct speech.[1] Now I have seen that many Jews pay no attention to our plain[2] language, much less to its obscure forms. Their style is therefore very faulty. Whenever they write poetry, the elements of the former are sparse, but the latter many, and when they rhyme, the speech becomes unintelligible and foolish. For this reason I found it necessary to write a book in which I gathered all vocables into two groups, the one containing every word according to the order of the alphabet, and similarly in parallel columns all the rhymes so that they may be easily learnt by heart, both the plain and obscure parts of the language. This book I wrote at the *age of twenty*, believing that it would enable the student to take from the first column what suited him best for the purposes of diction and rhyme. When several years after the publication of this book I noticed that students, in spite of my having settled text and rhymes for them, wanted me to tell them something of the burdens of poetry, I added them to the book. These burdens form the core of the poems, being guarded on either side by two columns. Though these categories and burdens be many, they are based on three principles, one of which embraces the parts of every speech, viz. *first*, call, question, statement, command, and stipulation; *second*, descriptions, forming four classes defined according to either matter, form, action, or completion, as I shall fully explain; *third*, classes of comparison, being similar to group two, with the difference that those refer to the object of comparison while the latter are taken from the result. These three principal groups shall be followed by many other chapters necessary for the poets. Wherever I found it necessary to quote examples by Jōsē b. Jōsē, Jannai,[3] El'āzar,[4] Joshua,[5] Phineas,[6] I did so. As regards the poets nearer our own time, I will confine myself to praise where it is due, but nothing to the contrary. I left the Hebrew Introduction as I first wrote it, placing it at the head of the book, but I felt constrained to translate it [into Arabic], because I saw the people's need of it. When I shall

[1] e g. Ta'lab's كتاب الفصيح, ed. Barth.

[2] Harkawy, ibid., *prophetic*, but the word means *inelegant.*

[3] See Davidson, *Mahzor Yannai*, New York, 1919.

[4] Kallir.

[5] Cp. Zunz, *Literaturgesch. der Synag. Poesie*, p. 459.

[6] Zunz, *Zur Gesch.* 474.

have copied the two columns that I have compiled I will fix the meanings and add them. I hope that, as I expect to help my readers with my book, so God will help me in my endeavours.

If any further proof be needed to establish the authenticity of this preface it is fully demonstrated by the manner in which the writer strengthens his point by quotations from the Bible. Sa'adyāh's bent for linguistic pursuits found opportunities on later occasions, especially in his collection of twelve grammatical treatises which he united into a volume under the title *Books of Languages*. This is no longer extant, except a brief extract inserted in his commentary on the *Book of Creation*, in which he discusses the treatment of the guttural letters in their various places in words, and the changes in their vocalization whenever required on account of their refusal to be doubled. Of special interest also is his endeavour to establish some crude rules of phonology, in which he had no guide, as the guttural letters enjoy no special privileges in Arabic. He notices the differences in the pronunciation of Hebrew between the Jews of Babylon and Palestine, but, unfortunately, gives no particulars. These *Books of Languages* fully justify their title, since they seem in their way to have furnished almost a whole grammar. This, of course, should not be understood in the sense of modern requirements, as much of it is merely mechanical, because the law of triliterality of roots remained unknown to him, as well as to the following generation. He seems, however, to have possessed a correct notion of the double pronunciation of the six consonants,[1] since a dissertation on them, styled *Book of Dāghēsh and Rāphé*, is mentioned in the commentary just alluded to, and formed a part of the *Books of Languages*.

Grammatical comments are also interspersed in Sa'adyāh's commentaries on the books of the Bible. In his commentary on Leviticus [2] there occurs the remark: 'A phrase is

[1] בגדכפת.

[2] See my article, *JQR.*, 1906, p. 20.

either a question, or a statement, command, prohibition, request, or vocative. Since it is clear that the character of each of these classes differs from that of the others, only an ignorant person, unfamiliar with the rules of speech, can mix up statement with command.' This remark, which recalls one contained in the Preface just reproduced, strengthens its authenticity.

Another and even more scientific attempt in the direction of lexicography is Sa'adyāh's glossary of *Ninety Words* which occur only once in the Bible.[1] His method of interpreting them consists in quoting parallel passages from the Mishnāh and Talmud. The arrangement of this glossary is not systematic in any way. Yet by drawing upon post-biblical material he gave the first impulse to Hebrew dialectology. To several words the Arabic translation is added. In illustration of his method two examples will serve. The words וילך שפי (Num. 23. 3) are explained by the quotation from the Talmud ובשופי [בקושי] (Niddāh 38 v°.) *with tranquillity*. A similar translation is given in his Arabic version of the Pentateuch. The word חולש (Isa. 14. 12) is explained by מטילין חלשין (Sabbath 149 v°.), *cast lots*, and the same translation appears in his commentary of Isaiah. At what period of his life this essay was composed is uncertain, but it looks like a compilation of notes accumulated while he was engaged in his translations. The close acquaintance it betrays with nearly all parts of the Talmud, Midrash, and the Targums tends to show that its final redaction belongs to his riper years.

QIRQISĀNI.

Hitherto unrecognized as a grammarian was the Qaraite Abu Joseph Ya'qūb al Qirqisāni,[2] a younger contemporary of Sa'adyāh, and probably a fellow student at the colleges of Baghdād. He has left no special work on grammar, but

[1] Only *seventy*, see the editions.
[2] See my *Qirqisāni Studies*, London, 1919.

the Introduction to his Arabic commentary on the Pentateuch, which has fortunately been preserved, contains a number of paragraphs devoted to grammatical research. Although they are merely given as aids to exegesis, they are too pronounced to be left unrecorded. The mutilated state in which the text has come down to us does not permit us to do full justice to his philological endeavours, but they reveal great proficiency, and likewise show that he was trained in the method of the Arabs. As a sample may serve his discussion of the etymology of the particle את by comparing it to its Arabic parallel *iyya*.[1] The Arabic method is further illustrated by his not separating rules of morphology from those of syntax. As regards the latter, he shows that a number of sentences should be re-arranged differently from the Masoretic text in order to give a logical sense. He discusses the use of collective nouns as plural ideas, and of real plural ones as singular notions.[2] He shows by a number of instances in which a negative particle placed at the beginning of a sentence extends its force to the second clause; further interrogative sentences in which the interrogative particle is omitted. He then discusses the transformation of the past tense of verbal forms into the future, and vice versa. He also dilates on the so-termed objective complement of the verb, redundant or defective words or constructions, &c.

However incomplete this work is, it suffices to show that Qirqisāni had a deep insight into the fabric of the Hebrew language. Of special interest it is to observe that Ibn Janāḥ,[3] who compiled his grammar a century later, employed exactly the same method, although it is hardly probable that he ever saw Qirqisāni's notes. In several instances the latter drew on the Targum, as e.g. in his comments on Exod. 23. 5; Num. 16. 27. In other instances he agrees with Saʿadyāh, for whose exegesis he seems to have entertained admiration, in spite of his strong

[1] Ibid., p. 32.

[2] Ibid., p. 33 sq.

[3] See farther on.

Qaraite antagonism. In any case, he represents the best type of Qaraite scholarship, and also as grammarian he deserves a place next to Saʿadyāh.

JUDAH B. QOREISH of Tahort in North Africa, was a physician who flourished in the middle of the tenth century. He left a work written in the form of an epistle in Arabic, addressed to the Jews of Fās (Fez), warning them not to neglect the study of the Targum to the Torāh. The work is divided into three parts. The *first* deals with the relation of Hebrew to Aramaic; the *second* treats on alleged post-biblical words occuring in the Bible; while the *third* is devoted to a discussion on the relation of Arabic to Hebrew. As his prefatory remarks reveal his aim clearly, and permit an insight into the comparatively forward state of philological research, I reproduce it here in translation:[1]

I have noticed that you discontinue the customary recitation of the Aramaic Targum to the Pentateuch in your synagogues in view to its being abandoned by the unlearned amongst you, who maintain that they do not require this translation, and yet understand the whole Hebrew language. Some of your people even remarked to me that they never read the Targum to the Pentateuch or to the Prophets. The Targum—God be good to you—has never been neglected by your forbears, much less abolished. Your scholars never left off teaching it, nor did your patriarchs do without it. Your ancestors were not ignorant of its use, and those who preceded you in Irāq (Babylon), Egypt, Africa, and Spanien were not remiss in making it known. When I mentioned to one of those who fight shy of the Targum that the Pentateuch contained some strange expressions, and that Hebrew was intermixed with Aramaic words, and had spread it like branches on trees and like veins in bodies, he was much roused, and greatly stimulated. He understood how helpful the Targum would be, and how much it would further the satisfactory explanation and clear comprehension of the text. He regretted to have missed studying it, and deplored the loss to him of this attractive idiom.

[1] See Bargès, *Epistola R. Jehuda b. Koreisch*, Paris, 1857.

I, therefore, resolved to write this book for intelligent readers that they may know that Aramaic and Arabic words, nay foreign and even Berber expressions are intermixed with the holy tongue, but Arabic in particular. For Arabic contains many words which we find to be pure Hebrew. In this respect there is between Hebrew and Arabic no other difference than the change of צ and צ̇, ג and ג̇, ט and ט̇, ע and ע̇, ח and כ̇, ד and ד̇. The cause of this resemblance and (consequent) interchange is to be found in the propinquity of habitations and consanguinity of races. Terah, the father of Abraham, was an Aramaean, just as Laban, while Ishmael and Kedar were Mostarabs[1] from the period of the Dispersion in Babel. Abraham, Isaac, and Jacob, however, adhered to the holy tongue which they inherited from Adam.[2] Now this language became mixed in consequence of infiltration, as we observe in every country which is neighboured by another with a different language, that transfusion and borrowing of words take place. For this reason we find resemblances between Hebrew and Arabic apart from the natural kinship of the consonants used for structural purposes in the beginning, the middle, and ends of words. Hebrew, Aramaic, and Arabic are by nature fashioned on one form, as we shall explain, if God so will it, in its place at the end of the book. We will begin by giving an account of Aramaic elements in the Tōrah, then of such rare words as can only be explained from the language of the Mishnāh, the Talmud, and finally of Arabic words. We will also explain those kindred consonants which in Hebrew, Aramaic, and Arabic stand in the beginning, in the middle, and at the end of words, but in no other language than these three. All these we will put down in alphabetical order, so that every letter wanted can easily be found in its place.

It is not overstating the case if we style Ibn Qoreish the father of comparative Semitic philology, although such observation is spontaneous rather than founded on his scientific comprehension of the grammatical structure of the three languages. In this respect he surpassed his Arab teachers, who confined their linguistic studies to the most

[1] Arabicized north Semites.

[2] The old Jewish tradition, cp. *Kitāb Al-khazari*, p. 124.

minute elaboration of the rules of their own language without acknowledging the existence of the kindred tongues. The law of triliterality, however, remained unknown to Ibn Qoreish, as well as to all Jewish grammarians of his and the next generations. To get over this difficulty he and others established the etymology of a noun or verb not by digging into the root, but by the quotation of parallels in which the meaning of the word in question was to be unmistakably given. The following is an example from Chapter I:

לכפן Targum כפנא *hunger* (Job 5. 22), but not to be compared to כפנה (Ezek. 17. 7), which is like כנף (*wing*), formed by transposition of consonants like כשב and כבשה, &c.

Nearly half of the first chapter is unfortunately missing. Chapter II discusses words which he considered to be post-biblical, and explains them by quotations from the Mishnāh and the Talmud, which, of course, is unjustified. From this and many other instances it can be seen that Ibn Qoreish's work is not merely a dry catalogue of alleged foreign words in the Bible, but it also assists exegesis. This is strikingly illustrated by an instance which runs as follows (p. 46):

They overlaid Jerusalem with beams (Neh. 3. 8). This is the explanation of ויעזבו, viz. They covered the houses with rafters, as in the Mishnāh (B. Mes. 10. 1) *a beam and a sleeper*, putting down wooden joists, as in Cant. 1. 17; 2 Kings 6. 5. The pattern on the planks and boards of the ceiling is called (in the Mishnāh) מעזיבה in contradistinction to Neh. 3. 8; 2 Sam. 5. 21; Gen. 39. 6, &c.

The third chapter deals with Hebrew and Arabic roots either identical or sharing one or two cognate consonants. In an appendix the author treats on the interchange of consonants in Hebrew, Arabic, and Aramaic. He shows the common features they have in the inflexion of verbs, illustrating the rules by numerous instances. He discusses the nature of the sibilants, and the causes of their frequent interchanges, and passes on to the conjugation of the past tense. Speaking of the prepositions, including מ, he shows the difference in the employment of ל in Hebrew and Arabic, amply illustrating this by examples. Finally, he explains some foreign words which he sought to discover in the Bible, even drawing on Berber vocabulary.

Dūnāsh b. Tamīm.

Abu Sahl Dūnāsh b. Tamīm Al Shafalji was a native of Kairwān in North Africa, a contemporary of Sa'adyāh, and a friend and perhaps a pupil of the famous physician and philosopher Isaac Al Isrāili, the elder. Of his life we know nothing, and not much more of the practical interest he took in linguistic pursuits, and this on second-hand evidence. Ibn Ezra in his brief survey of early Jewish grammarians,[1] mentions a work from his pen, but all he says is that it was a mixture of Hebrew and Arabic. It is possible that this remark refers to the commentary on the Sēpher Yeṣīrāh with which he is credited, and which offered much scope for grammatical discussion. More definite are the statements of Moses b. Ezra, who quotes his name on about twenty occasions[2] in his work on Poetics. One of these passages is a comment on Isa. 11.14. He is further alluded to in the commentary on the first Book of Samuel by Tanḥūm of Jerusalem.[3] Finally, Sa'adyāh b. Danān,[4] a Spanish author of the sixteenth century, reports on the authority of Moslem authors that Dūnāsh embraced Islām. Had this been the case, the Jewish authors mentioned before would have ignored him.[5]

David b. Abraham.

In the meanwhile the study of the Hebrew language had found a new home as far west as Morocco, and in

1 In his *Mòznayim*, see later on.

2 See Kokovzov, *Kitāb Al Muḥāḏara*, Petrograd, 1895, pp. 212–15; Munk, *Notice sur Abou'l Walid*, pp. 43–60.

3 See farther on.

4 See farther on p. 96.

5 Especially Ibn Ezra, whose son embraced Islām.

a new Qaraite adept and youngest of Saʿadyāh's contemporaries, called David b. Abraham. He composed a dictionary in Arabic, likewise styled *Agron*, in which he grouped all Hebrew words in four classes according to the number of what he considered radical letters, beginning with those consisting of one only. Such was the primitive point of view shared by all grammarians of this and the following periods, which clung to the notion that only strong consonants formed a root, while the disappearance of weak radicals in certain forms had not yet been recognized. David b. Abraham [1] acknowledged only words of one, two, three, and four letters. Proper names of more than four letters he considered exceptions. This dictionary has come down to us in very defective form. To judge from a remark at the end of the preface, the author also seems to have compiled a grammar. We also gather that he followed the Tiberian system of vocalization.[2] It is therefore probable that he was trained either in a Palestinian school or by Palestinian teachers, and, indeed, a copy of the work was preserved in the Qaraite Synagogue in Jerusalem, and brought to Europe by the late Dr. Neubauer.[3] Prior to this extracts were published mostly in Hebrew translation by S. Pinsker.[4] To illustrate this author's method I here insert the translation of one of the paragraphs which Pinsker reproduces in the Arabic original:

Root זל, in Arabic דל, with interchange of *zain* with *dāl*, as in Lam. 1. 8 *they despised her*, as also Jer. 15. 19 *if thou take forth a precious one from the vile thou shalt be as my word*, which means: 'when thou hast made the wicked one better, and hast led him on to piety, thou shalt be as I have promised thee (v. 20), and I will make thee unto this people as a *fencing brazen* wall.' Likewise זלות (Ps. 12. 9), 'removal of the baseness of the children of man', here alludes to Israel. Similarly Lam. 1. 11, which means: 'Thou hast become a base and vile woman.' The poet

[1] Cp. *JA.*, 1861, p. 471. [2] Ibid., p. 476. [3] Ibid.
[4] Liqqūṭē *Qadm.*, p. 144.

here alludes to her eating the flesh of children, as in Deut. 28. 53, but the former explanation is more acceptable. The word זולל refers to the debased woman, because her husband is held in contempt. A person often becomes low on account of his high station (?), and for this reason he is called זולל, because he is in reality low-minded. The intelligent person is high-minded, and takes no pleasure in anything vile, as in Prov. 17. 27 (יקר). In Arabic the same root is used in the sense of 'ceasing to be in a certain position', because *Arabic is closely related* to הזלים (Isa. 46. 6), which means: 'They remove the gold from the bag and spend it on things by which God will not allow him to profit.'

David b. Abraham constructs the following crude classification of Hebrew words: (1) Words standing independently in their meaning, e.g. *he shall hear* (ישמע); homonyms; (2) words which give no sense unless some letters change their places;[1] (3) words which require an additional letter,[2] or the omission of one;[3] (4) words unaffected by a redundant or missing letter;[4] (5) plural forms with singular meaning; (6) words with two adjectives, one masculine, the other feminine,[5] or masculine forms with feminine meaning, or masculine forms with feminine termination; (7) words with a one-letter suffix, or followed by a pronoun in accusative; (8) passive forms expressing future actions, and vice versa. Other words without cognate forms in the Bible, but in the Talmud ('the language of the Ancient'). Other words that can only be explained from Syriac or Arabic.

David b. Abraham's comparative method resembles that of Ibn Qoreish (whom he occasionally quotes) in so far as both consider the Syriac and Arabic words to which they refer as borrowed from Hebrew. We gather from his words that the Jewish grammarians of the period, although in their exegesis often surprisingly original, groped in the dark in matters grammatical. The treatment of the weak

[1] e.g. קהלת, Deut. 33. 4, and להקת, 1 Sam. 19. 20.
[2] מכות for מכלת, 2 Chron. 2. 9.
[3] Ezek. 8. 16.
[4] Exod. 29. 35.
[5] 1 Kings 19. 11.

consonants in particular remained a mystery to them, and prevented their real understanding of roots containing one or two of such consonants. There is sufficient dissimilarity in this respect between Hebrew and Arabic to act as a barrier, while the intricacies of the Hebrew irregular verb are incomparably more perplexing than in Arabic. It was perhaps the recognition of the unsatisfactory character of this comparative method which led to a reaction that a decade or two later took place in Spain, where, under the patronage of the famous statesman Ḥisdāi b. Shaphrūt, Jewish learning had found a new home.

CHAPTER II

Menaḥem b. Saruq, Dūnāsh b. Labrat.

Menaḥem discarded Arabic entirely, and is therefore the first Jewish grammarian who wrote in Hebrew. The fruit of his labours is a dictionary, and in its completeness the first of its kind known to us. It bears the title *Maḥbereth Menaḥem*,[1] and embraces the whole Hebrew and Aramaic vocabulary of the Bible. In consequence of the use of Hebrew exclusively the author was forced to create a new grammatical terminology, but the style is clear and concise, and not without originality. As to his insight into the inner working of the Hebrew language he did not go beyond his forerunners. In the brief introduction which deals with the classification and function of consonants, the author adheres to the theory of roots consisting of one letter, but remained ignorant of any difference between strong and weak consonants. Like Saʿadyāh (to whom he alludes twice) he divides the twenty-two letters of the alphabet into two groups of eleven each. One of these groups contains consonants which in his opinion only occur as radical, but never as accessory letters. He also briefly alludes to the rules concerning the hard or soft pronunciation of the *begadkephath*, and the peculiarity of the gutturals. The vowels are mentioned without any further discussion of their nature and function. The whole material is arranged alphabetically, but as the author failed to recognize weak roots most words are arranged quite mechanically according to their external appearance. In consequence words with widely different etymologies are placed in the same paragraph. Menaḥem gives speci-

[1] ed. Filipowski, London, 1854.

mens of roots with two radicals, and a complete list of such with only one radical, and also of words which only occur once in the Bible. The following extracts will aptly illustrate his scientific standpoint, as well as his method. They are taken from the section of the letter *aleph*:

Ehyeh (Exod. 3. 14) is the holy, honoured, and awe-inspiring name. This word has no derivation from any other word. Interpreters say it is derived from the (same) stem (as) הויה, יהיו, לחיות. Their meaning seems to be: God said to Moses, *I am that I am*, as if He had said: I was from eternity, I am now, and I shall be for ever. But in the repetition of the word in the passage, *ĕhyĕh has sent me to you*, the interpretations of the word are divided, so that it becomes like one of those words which have no explanation, or like a name that has no derivation from any (other) word. For the [nature of the] initial *aleph* prevents it belonging to a stem in the latter quotation. It, therefore, cannot be like *ĕhyĕh* in Hos. 14. 6; 2 Sam. 7. 14; Exod. 3. 12. If this were not the case I would not have included this word in the section of *aleph*.

אר has seven divisions. (1) Gen. 1. 3; Ps. 119. 130; Gen. 1. 15; Ezek. 32. 8 referring to the sun. (2) Cant. 5. 1; Ps. 80. 13; Isa. 27. 11 (*gathering*). (3) Judges 5. 23; Mal. 3. 9; Num. 23. 7 (*cursing*). (4) Neh. 9. 7; Isa. 24. 15; 11. 8 referring to valleys, clefts, and rocks. The word חר (ibid.) points to the preceding *hole of the asp*. Thus אור כשדים means *the valley of the Chaldeans*, as can be seen from Gen. 11. 28. (5) Exod. 14. 20; Ps. 139. 11; Job 37. 11, which *may be* like ויחרגו, Ps. 18. 46, and ועצמו.[1] Jer. 50. 17. (6) 2 Kings 4. 39; Isa. 18. 4 (*herbs*). (7) Exod. 28. 30. An eighth division is devoted to Aramaic, viz. Dan. 7. 5, 13, which is to be explained: *they were*.

We call a work epoch-making when it opens up new paths, creates ideas, stimulates men's minds, leads to fruitful discussion, and promotes further development of the initial effort. In this sense Menaḥem's work with all its imperfections marks the beginning of a new era in the study of Hebrew. To Jews outside the Arabic-speaking

[1] Misprint in ed.

world in Asia and Europe the dictionary came as a timely adviser in their studies of the Bible. It became rapidly popular in Spain, France, and Italy, and, as is well known, Rashi, Ibn Ezra, and later lexicographers quote it frequently. Its immediate effect was that it gave rise to one of the most stirring, nay fascinating, episodes in Jewish literature, introducing new names, of which the first is that of

Dūnāsh b. Labrat.[1]

This interesting personality re-establishes the link with Babylon, Maghreb, and Spain. He was a native of Fās, but studied at Baghdād, which was the original home of his family. Here, as we are informed, he was a pupil of Sa'adyāh, but there is every likelihood that at the same time he attended the lectures of some Arab professor of grammar, for which discipline Baghdād was a famous centre. He seems to have given special attention to Arabic poetry, because he was the first Jew who attempted to adapt the laws of Arab poetry to Hebrew verse. Now we should remark here at once that the nature of the short open syllable in Arabic bears a quite different aspect in Hebrew, so that simple transference of Arab rules into Hebrew is impossible, Hebrew using the *shᵉwā mobile* in the place of a short vowel. Apart from this the Arabic foot (the smallest consisting of two syllables) is cut up into smaller units for Hebrew purposes. The way in which Dūnāsh wrought this adaptation is exceedingly ingenious, and although its employment in Hebrew is at variance with important rules of phonology, the practice soon became popular, and the best poets in Spain and Italy adopted it without demur.

Having completed his studies Dūnāsh returned to his native country, and lived subsequently in Spain. Equipped with a profound knowledge of Hebrew, and endowed with

[1] The etymology of this word is somewhat obscure, probably أَدُونَش, cp. *JA*. XVI, p. 27.

incisive critical powers, he soon detected many weak points in Menaḥem's dictionary, and lost no time in publishing corrections in a long poem, Arabic in form, with the modification that the two half-lines are again divided so that the first three sections show an inner rhyme, while the main rhyme is carried through all the final sections, thus forming quatrains. The first forty lines contain a eulogy addressed to Ḥisdaī. This is followed by several lines of praise for Menaḥem, who through the rest of the poem is exposed to merciless criticism. These poetic criticisms are supplemented by detailed discussions in prose, the latter preceded by an introduction in which the author gives a sketch of the scholastic requirements of a grammarian. Sa'adyāh's influence is here strongly conspicuous. For just like him Dūnāsh interprets the sentence to be divided into *five* classes, viz. statement, query, exclamation, command, and request. There is, however, a marked progress visible in Dūnāsh's notes. He knows of three tenses: past, imperfect, and future, which looks as if he had borrowed from a Latin grammar book. His grouping of the consonants is more scientific than that of any of his predecessors, he being the first to put the four weak consonants into a special group. He speaks of the use of ה as definite article as well as interrogative particle. This was, however, already known to Qirqisāni. He also betrays some insight into the fact of the disappearance of certain verbal forms with one of the weak letters (ו and י), which share the same fate in Arabic, yet he fell short of penetrating into the secret of the irregular verb as a whole. He was therefore scarcely justified in concluding his Introduction with the arrogant expressions hurled against the 'erring but unoffending Menaḥem': 'Thou didst,' he says, 'mock at wise men, open thy mouth wide against them, make thy friends mourn, and thy enemies glad. I will heal what thou hast injured, and fence up what thou has shattered by the interpretation of my poem.'

The following may serve as an illustration of Dūnāsh's

criticism. Menaḥem had put the word בנס (Aramaic part of Dan. 2. 12) into the section of the letter ב, to which it really belongs. Dūnāsh, however, quite mistakenly apostrophizes him in the following manner:

Thou hast put בנס under ב, but it belongs to נ, the meaning of the passage being *in anger and rage*, as Targum to Gen. 40. 6 shows. If thou object to this on account of the ו in the following ואמר, I rejoin that this ו is a mere detail for which there are many parallel passages, as Isa. 23. 3; 2 Sam. 13. 20; Gen. 36. 24; Dan. 8. 13; 9. 25; Hab. 2. 6; Ps. 76. 7; Ezek. 47. 11; 2 Chron. 13. 10,[1]—so understand, and go out of darkness into light.

אנך (Amos 7. 7). Thou hast said that the א is not radical, and comparest it to נכים (Ps. 35. 15), and explainst it: *as walls which he has pulled down and broken up.* It is senseless to say 'a wall of destruction', or 'a wall of building', or 'a wall of iron'. אנך means *lead* as in Arabic, and would thus be suitable to stand in construct state (with *the wall*). In the passage quoted an object is meant which can be seized with the hand, and it is known that plummets are made of lead and suspended on a line. The prophet expresses the same ideas as in Isa. 28. 17; Lam. 2. 8.

סלסלות (Jer. 6. 9). Thou hast compared this word to Gen. 40. 17 (*basket*), but they have nothing in common with one another, for baskets are receptacles and vessels, while סַלְסִלּוֹת are *branches*. The verse in question serves as a reminder to examine the grapes and branches once more, and to glean them. As in סַלֵּי (Gen. 40. 16) it only has one ל, as also in גַלֵּי הַיָּם (Isa. 48. 18), the ל cannot be repeated, we cannot change סלים into סלסלות or סלסלים.

The rudeness of Dūnāsh's tone was perhaps prompted by professional jealousy, but possibly also by natural disposition. For Menaḥem it had a fatal consequence, for it cost him the protection of Ḥisdai, and darkened the declining years of his life. Less intelligible is the same tone in which Dūnāsh indulges in a subsequent criticism of a number of Sa'adyāh's interpretations. This criticism has come down to us in a number of incoherent notes, of which the following are specimens:

[1] Dūnāsh, p. 10.

זרים (Isa. 1. 7) is explained by Sa'adyāh as *shower*, as if it were the plural of זרם and similar nouns, but it should be as Joel 4. 17, viz. *strangers*, the passage in Isaiah having a meaning similar to Deut. 29. 22. Be careful, my son, in the interpretation of the Tōrāh, and let the fear of God be upon thee.

כַּדּוּר (Isa. 22. 18) is like כִּידוֹר (Job 15. 24). The latter word is quinqueliteral, so both do not resemble one another in form or meaning. כַּדּוּר is triliteral, the כ being added, but in כידור it is radical. A striking proof of this is found in the Mishnāh—it is laid down:

An *ethrōg* כַּדּוּר *is unlawful*, i.e. round on all sides. Were the כ radical they would have said ככדור. The meaning of כידור is *camp*. Hear my son and understand.

These specimens of Dunash's attacks against Menaḥem, as well as other paragraphs, are not without their weak points,[1] which did not escape the notice of Menaḥem's disciples. Three of them took up the cudgels on behalf of their master, and composed an anonymous rejoinder. Their names were subsequently disclosed in the reply published by Dūnāsh's pupils, viz. Ephraim b. Kaphron, Judah b. David, and Isaac b. Chiqatilla. They, too, addressed themselves to Ḥisdai, mildly hinting at the injustice he allowed Menaḥem to suffer. 'I know', their spokesman[2] said 'that there is no injustice in his (Ḥisdai's) tent, truth is his lot, but neither vanity nor falsehood. He who speaks lies finds no favour with him, but he delights in justice and loves righteousness. My heart is roused to answer and render clear the word of him who conducts himself as lord over all the intepreters, viz. the son of Labrat, who precipitated himself into falsity, yet imagines that he is the master of interpretation. He has destroyed the remnant of the holy language by measuring it with the measurement of strangers which plays havoc with the vowels.'

[1] See Jacob Tām's rejoinder.

[2] Probably Judah b. David.

In order to show that Dūnāsh was not the only Jewish adept in Arabic prosody, they composed their rejoinder in exactly the same form and with the same rhyme as their opponents, and made this the first line of attack. They pointed out that Hebrew differs from Arabic in the build of the syllable. For while the latter permits the sequence of two open and short syllables, this is not possible in Hebrew, in which a final short syllable is dropped, every word ending in a consonant, or at least a quiescent letter which lengthens the syllable. They illustrate this by quoting some other verses of Dūnāsh in which he apparently had applied the rules of Arabic prosody, inserting irregular short syllables at the end of two words,[1] and opening or closing syllables at will. 'Sa'adyāh also', they continue, 'composed many poems with rhymes, but he did not follow Arab models. Thou, however, who at that time wert the most important of his disciples, didst not profit from the mind of the greatest of thy teachers. . . . Had he found that Arab prosody might be applied to Hebrew he would have preceded thee and not thou him. For he was aware that it is improper to do so and to destroy the language, and to play loose with the long and short vowels and the rules of grammar. . . . What induced me to produce a metrical poem was to show thee that the practice is easy. Now let not thy heart be proud thinking "who can do so beside me"; for since thou art not equal to the task, thou hast corrupted the language. This is no secret art, for had we wished to spoil the holy tongue as thou hast done, we could write in Arabic metres, as well as our children, &c.'

They then continue in prose to demolish one after the other of Dūnāsh's criticisms, interrupting their remarks by inserting several paragraphs in which they point out

[1] This point is not quite clear. The verse in question read without these alleged additional short syllables corresponds to the Arabic metre *ramal*, but the poet took the liberty of transforming the *shᵉwā quiescent* of דִּמְ into *shᵉwā mobile*, thus *dimᵉōth*. Similar instances are quite common in the poems of the Spanish school.

Dūnāsh's errors in fashioning words which are mere corruptions of Biblical models. This offers an opportunity of discussing various classes of segholate nouns in connexion with the tone-syllable, and to disclose Dūnāsh's mistakes. This sharp anti-criticism furnished Dūnāsh's pupils with weapons to defend their master. One of them, Judah b. Shēsheth, undertook this task in a poem kept again in the same form and rhyme with interposed prose explanations. He even surpasses his predecessors in acrimonious language, and does not even refrain from personal invective. It was specially the name of Kaphron which tickled his particular sense of humour, as he derived it from the Latin *caper*, 'a goat', and indulged in facetious allusions to this animal's bleating. In defence of the employment of Arab metres by Dūnāsh he quotes a number of places in the Bible where the Jewish Masoretes themselves indulged in a certain laxity in the matter of open and closed syllables.[1] Poets therefore commit no wrong if they follow their example.

There is no need to enter more fully into this controversy, especially as the fighters on both sides had but insufficient knowledge of the true nature of the weak Hebrew roots, which forms one of the most arduous difficulties in the study of this language. Yet it shows the advanced state of their general training, which must have included the study of classics. Apart from this the struggle had a very important consequence, as it stimulated further research, and finally led to the discovery of truth. The most remarkable point is that it was a member of the vanquished party who was responsible for this achievement, as we shall see later on.

[1] By the use of the so-called *sh^ewā medium*.

CHAPTER III

Jepheth b. Aliy.

In the period immediately following that of Saʿadyāh we find the study of the Hebrew language also spreading to Jerusalem, and its earliest representative was, as far as we know at present, the famous Qaraite Jepheth. There exists no special work by him on this subject, but his bulky commentaries on the books of the Bible are interspersed with grammatical and lexicographical discussions. A number of them have been extracted by the late Solomon Munk, and published with French translation.[1] I here reproduce two short paragraphs:

אמילם (Ps. 118. 11) is derived from the same root as יִמָּל (Job 14. 2) יִמַּל (ibid. 18, 16) the *pataḥ* of which stands for אֲמִילֵם like אֲשִׁימֵם. One grammarian translates אמילם ‘I shall cut them’, without the suffix, because he takes the ם as a radical letter.

אל ראי אחרי ראי (Gen. 16. 13): we must explain the rule of these two expressions; ראי is like עֳנִי עמי (Exod. 3. 7) and the absolute forms are רֹאִי, עֳנִי, as in Nahum 3. 6, Deut. 16. 3—*omnipotent of sight*. As to רֹאִי it is like עֹשִׂי, קֹנִי which I translate: *He who sees me.*

To his commentary on Hosea, Jepheth added an appendix in explanation of specially difficult passages. It is of sufficient interest to be reproduced in translation:[2]

I must mention difficult words in this book which I translated and show their derivations and grammatical forms so that the student may, if God so will it, dwell upon them. שָׂךְ (2. 8) is of the same root as מְשׂוּכָּתוֹ (so, Isa. 5. 5), the imperative being שֹׂךְ as קם, קום, ישב.—אֶתְנָה (ibid. 14) is like אתנן, the first נ being radical while the second is additional, which is also the case with ה in

[1] *JA.* XV, p. 314.

[2] See Appendix I.

אתנה.—וַתַּעַד (ibid. 15) has imperative עֲדֵה, but the ה is missing in וַתַּעַשׂ וַתַּעַל.—In מְפַתֶּיהָ (ibid. 16) the ׳ is redundant. The verbal noun of וָאֶכְּרֶהָ (3. 2) may be נכר as נצר and אצרך (Jer. 1. 5), or הכר with *ḥāṭēph*, but defective spelling. If it were like ואכירה, the verbal noun would have ׳ as in ותחילנה,[1] the verbal noun of which is החל, הסר as in ואכרה.[2]—וְדָמִיתִי (4. 5) has imperative דְּמֵה[3]. The latter word has two explanations, the first being like דְּמֵה (Cant. 2. 17), the other having the meaning of *silence* as in Hosea.—הֵבוּ (4. 18), imp. sing. הָבָה, plur. הָבוּ as in זרו (Zech. 2. 4). —צָרַר (ibid. 19) allows the two explanations of *oppressing* and *binding*. I chose the latter as in Exod. 12. 34, the verbal noun צְרוֹר as שְׁמוֹר.—In שִׁכְמָה (6. 9) the ה is redundant, because שֶׁכֶם (*shoulder*) is meant as in Job 31. 36; 1 Sam. 9. 2.—The ׳ in שערוריה (v. 10) is added as in הומיה, בוכיה, the form being שערורה. —In בֹּעֲרָה (7. 4) the ה is redundant, because the tone is on the ע[4]; were it *millerā* it would be feminine, but I took it as masculine and not feminine.—The root of הֶחֱלוּ (v. 5) is חלה. I therefore translated *they rendered ill*, but not *they were ill*, the meaning being that the princes made the king ill.—The meaning of אַיְסִרֵם (v. 12) is *I chastise them*, the imperative being הַיְסֵר like הַשְׁמֵד, of which אַשְׁמִידֵם is derived.—יִתְגּוֹרָרוּ (v. 14) is derived from גור (1 Kings 17. 20), imperative התגוררו.—The meaning of לֹא עָל (v. 16) is *high*, as in 2 Sam. 23. 1. Others explain it *made useful*, as in Jer. 2. 8.—בּוֹקֵק (10. 1) is not like Isa. 24. 1, which I translate *the enemy has destroyed it*, but not ביר.—חלק (v. 2) is not as in Deut. 4. 19. I therefore translate *their heart has severed them*, but not *their heart was divided*.—יַעֲרֹף (ibid. has two explanations, the first being like Deut. 32. 2, the other like Deut. 21. 4 and Exod. 13. 13.— שְׁכַן (v. 5) is the construct state of שָׁכֵן, like זְקַן. The word has two explanations, (1) *neighbour*, Jer. 12. 14; (2) *dweller*, like שֹׁכֵן, only the latter is a noun derived from the verb, which is not the case with שָׁכֵן, אָהֵב.—בָּשְׁנָה (v. 6) means *debasement*, the ב being redundant as in שִׁבְעָנָה (Job 42. 13). It may also be a noun.—נִדְמָה (v. 7) may be translated by *dumb*, or *compared* as the masculine of נִדְמָה, imperative הִדָּמֵה, but the feminine should be נִדְמְתָה.—כְּקֶצֶף (ibid.) is taken *like foam* on account of the

[1] MT. ותחלינה, Gen. 41. 54.
[2] The author was evidently puzzled by the *dagesh dirimens.*
[3] Dagesh is omitted in the MS. [4] See the Māsōrāh.

context, but not etymologically.—The singular of עונותם (v. 10) is עונה. There are *three* nouns [derived from the same root]. (1) מַעֲנָה (1 Sam. 14. 14), a *furrow*; (2) מַעֲנִית (Ps. 129. 3); (3) עוֹנָה (Exod. 21. 10) which is like Hosea.—אֹהַבְתִּי (v. 11) with י redundant, the meaning being *thou art loving*. Others translate *she who loves me*, with the י in its proper place.—נִדְמֹה (v. 15) is the verbal noun as in נִכְסֹף (Gen. 31. 30).—תִרְגַּלְתִּי (11. v. 3) is from תרגל, as in Arabic, to *put some one on his feet*.[1]—קָחָם (ibid.) is a noun, viz. *their taking*, but it lacks a past tense.—לְחֵיהֵם (v.4) *their freshness*, as in Ezek. 17. 24. If their meaning were *their cheekbones*, it should be לְחָיֵיהֶם.—וְאַט (ibid.) from הִטָּה, as in וָאַךְ אותך (Ex. 9. 15) from הִכָּה, the ה being omitted.—אוביל (ibid.) from[2] הוביל. —אלות (10. 4) *sins*, plur. of אָלָה, as שנה and שנות.—כְּרֹת (ibid.) is an infinitive-imperative כְּרוֹת, as שָׁמוֹר and שְׁמוֹר.—The imperative of וְחָלָה (11. 6) is חל, like ושבה (Isa. 23. 17) from שוב.—תלוּאים (v. 7) from תלָה, as קְרוּאִים from קרא, the א being a radical. I therefore translated *suspended*, but not *being behind*.—נִחוּמָי (v. 8) is the singular of נחום as בכוּר.—תַלְאוּבוֹת (13. 5) is the plural of תַּלְאוּבָה, which occurs nowhere else in the Bible.—קָטָבְךָ (v. 14) from קטב.—סְגוֹר (v. 8) may be a noun expressing the fat which is upon the heart, or an *infinitive* form, meaning the *closure of the heart*.—במשבר (v. 13) is the same as in Isa. 37. 3.—דבריך (v. 14) is from דֶּבֶר.—יפריא (v. 15) is like המרה and תמרי (Job 39. 18), the verbal noun being הַמְרֵה, cp. יפליא, ימציא, and the verbal noun of all these verbs has either א or י.

[1] تَرَجَّل, a denominative of رِجْل, *foot*.

[2] MT. אוביל.

CHAPTER IV.

Judah b. Ḥayyūj, Abul Walīd (b. Marwān) ibn Janāḥ.

Up to this period Hebrew linguistics was more or less the object of speculation. The first to replace it by true insight was Judah Ḥayyūj of Fās, a disciple of Menaḥem. It is now an established fact that he was the author of the rejoinder to Dūnāsh. This is all we know at present about this man, whom Abraham b. Ezra justly styles 'the First of Grammarians'. The treatise by which he placed Hebrew grammar on a scientific basis deals with roots of which one (or two) of the radicals is either *āleph*, *wāw*, or *yōd*. The discovery of the true character of these roots is practically identical with the solution of the riddle of the triliteral Hebrew root, in contradistinction to alleged roots of two, or even one, radicals which till then had puzzled all Jewish linguists, and caused many fallacious opinions. The reason why earlier students had failed to recognize this was probably their very intimacy with the Hebrew language, and consequent lack of perspective. This is not an isolated phenomenon. As for Ḥayyūj, two circumstances helped him along. The first was his close acquaintance with Arabic. The triliteral form of the roots of this language is much more conspicuous than in Hebrew, and had been recognized long before. Even in hollow roots the inaudible middle consonant is expressed orthographically by the letter of prolongation (*ā*), which, with very few exceptions, is absent in Hebrew. From the knowledge of the nature of roots consisting of three strong consonants to the examination of the weak ones was but one step, yet it required the sagacity of a genius to make this one step, and to discover that the long middle vowel in *qām* takes the place of the invisible radical letter. The second circumstance was the dispute with Dūnāsh. It stimulated deeper study, sharpened his acumen, and led to a more minute examination of the older theory.

To this state of things we owe the existence of a work consisting of three treatises, all written in Arabic. The first, which appears to have been adumbrated in his defence of Menaḥem, is styled *Book of Punctuation*, and is of masoretic as well as grammatical character. It deals with the vowels according to the nature of the consonants, the tone-syllable especially in segholate forms, and the position of the accent in the latter; further, the change of vowels caused by addition of suffixes. Triliterality of roots appears here as an established fact. The treatise must therefore be considered as the earliest attempt to place Hebrew phonology on a scientific basis.

In his poetic productions Menaḥem had moulded several forms which, in consequence of the law discovered by him, appeared to Ḥayyūj inadmissible. He discusses this somewhat broadly in the introduction to the *second* and principal treatise, which deals with roots containing one or more weak consonants.

My aim, he says, in the composition of this book is to explain the weak as well as the letters of prolongation in Hebrew, and to draw attention to their ways and changes which, on account of their weakness, anomaly, and abstruseness are unknown to many people. They are ignorant as to how to inflect such verbs, and introduce them into their speeches and poems in a faulty and rule-violating manner. Thus one of them (Menaḥem) forms צְרוֹתוֹ from יָצַר and לְעוֹד from עדה without noticing that both are impossible forms.[1] In this way the build of the language was mutilated, the rules were destroyed, and their walls broken down, because roots of which one of the radicals is weak were mixed with one another. When I became aware of this change I composed this book with the help of God, explaining in it the ways and changes of these letters as well as the occasions in which they

[1] See Ewald-Dukes Beiträge, iii, p. 1 (abridged.)

are either omitted or interchanged. Prior to this I explained why they are called weak and lengthening letters, the occasions of the absorption of a quiescent letter, and other matters that call for elucidation, and which I considered to be useful. For all these I relied on the text of the Bible and forms analogous to its vocabulary, though they do not actually occur. I mean to say that when I found one certain form of a verb without the remaining ones, I inferred the absent ones from the one occurring as long as no disturbing factor interfered. I compiled all the verbs concerned as they are found in the Bible, and arranged them accurately in classes and groups in order to attain my object in the most complete manner, and make my book, if it please God, as useful as possible. My aim in treating on my subject was not to indulge in elegant and poetic style, but rather to avoid any flaw in the meaning of what I intended to say, my intention being to make myself understood with all the means I have to express myself clearly. Haply the reader of this book will forbear finding fault here and there, if it please God. It is incumbent on us who ardently desire to study the grammar of this language to emulate the ancient Hebrews born and bred in it, let alone the language of Revelation and Prophecy. If we follow their lead in matters of the language, our language is built on its foundations. Its roots send forth branches, and we now know of the language what we did not know before, and derive profit from what we learn.

Ḥayyūj begins by explaining the nature of the vowel; he shows that no Hebrew word can begin with a vowelless consonant, or end[1] in a vowel. He then discusses the three weak consonants *āleph*, *wāw*, and *yōd*, their occasional disappearance, their power of softening the consonants with double pronunciation (*aspiration of tenues*), and their interchanges both in speech and writing.

The work is quite naturally divided into three sections according as one of the weak letters occupies the first, second, or third place, the first section being headed by a crude survey of the various conjugations, both strong

[1] lit. *without support.*

and weak verbs. The following is a specimen of the work (abridged):[1]

Verbs with י as first radical, e.g. יָרַד, יָשַׁב, יָצָא, יָדַע, if provided with one of the four formative letters (אית״ן) do not express the first radical orthographically, but have יֵרֵד (in imperfect), &c., the י having *ṣērē*, in order to point to the missing lengthening letter. Whoever reads differently betrays his ignorance of what is correct, because he drops the first radical entirely. In forms like יֵרְדוּ, &c. [the long vowel of the first syllable takes the place of the first radical, as does the ש in ישמעו].[2] To most people, as far as I see, the difference between וְיָדְעוּ and וַיֵּדְעוּ is invisible, although it is quite obvious. Some of them call it now a profound mystery, while others see no difference between these two forms. This is only because they do not see the י written, and do not grasp that it is retained in speech. I say that the י in וְיָדְעוּ is the first radical as you know [as in וְשָׁמְרוּ], because the past tense is יָדַע, plur. יָדְעוּ. If ו be added to the past tense it is either perfect or future, because this is permitted in Hebrew as in וּבָנוּ (Isa. 60. 10). The י in וַיֵּדְעוּ is not radical, the first radical being represented by the *ṣērē* of the first syllable. This form can therefore only be future. In the imperative the י is dropped, viz. רֵד, just as the imperative of יעץ is עוּץ (Isa. 8. 10).[3] This, however, is irregular, as it should be עַץ or עֵץ, according to the original form יְעַץ, like יְרָא (Prov. 3. 7) and יְצֹק (Ezek. 24. 3), which are the regular forms. Sometimes ה is added, as in רְדָה, דְּעָה (Prov. 24. 14), but the last-named can also be a noun. The infinitive adds ת in compensation of the omitted י, viz. רֶדֶת and צֵאת with quiescent א.

The third treatise deals with the verbs of double radicals. The author introduces his list by a discussion of their grammatical aspect in the sundry conjugations, and shows how the contracted forms were evolved from the uncontracted stems. In this he betrays a remarkable progress as compared with his predecessors. His list also includes roots from which no verbal forms but only nouns occur, as

[1] ibid., p. 58.

[2] The words between [ ] are missing in the Arabic original, and are taken from the Hebrew version.

[3] Cp. Kahle in *ZDMG*. 55, p. 168.

הַר, טַל, חֹק. The word בבל he derives from באבל, thus deviating from the biblical explanation.

There exists another work of Ḥayyūj, a rather large fragment of which is extant in Leningrad, and was published together with other fragments by Professor Paul Kokovzov in 1916. His Introduction and all the notes are written in Russian, and therefore not readily accessible. It is styled *Book of Notes*, but is restricted to the two Books of Kings, Isaiah, Jeremiah, and Ezekiel. I here insert two brief abstracts in translation:

They cut themselves after their manner (1 Kings 18. 28). I thought that this word [ויתגודדו] belonged to the class of the double radicals, as in Deut. 14. 1, till I saw Gen. 49. 19. For יְגוּדֶנּוּ and יָגוּד do not belong to the same root as גְּדוּד, because this word belongs to that class, while the others have a weak middle radical; but ויתגודדו is an intensive stem with a different meaning. This has remained unmentioned in the treatise on the weak radicals (p. 8).

The meaning of these words (צו לצו, &c., Isa. 28. 10) is that they are helpless and of little understanding as *babies just weaned*, for whom speech is broken up bit by bit and letter by letter judiciously. For those people the plain word of God is like language for infants broken up into small bits *that they may go and fall backward, and be broken* (v. 13). The two instances of 'construct state', as I have explained, is this. Hebrew uses this construction in connexion with the prepositions מ, ב, and ל, as in חמת מיין (Hos. 7. 5), &c. The (above-mentioned) words are expressions of mimicry which are used to make a child understand. The Prophet calls it צו because he uses them as a *command*, and instruction how to receive it. As to קו, it is employed by the Prophet in the sense of Isa. 18. 2, which is a metaphorical expression for the *measuring line*. Another possible explanation is that קו means 'signs' and 'lines' for some one, one after the other (p. 24).

This etymology is repeated in the paragraph on בלל, with the comment that the two words were united into one, which for this reason is written without the א like בָּגָד

(Gen. 30. 11), and contracted from באגד. In this way בבל is derived from בלל.

In the place of an extract from this treatise it will be sufficient to mention some items in which the author differs from the etymologies to be found in modern Hebrew lexicography.

The word נֵארים (Mal. 3. 9) he derives from נאר like נֵאֵר (Lam. 2. 7), rejecting אור. This is contracted from ננארים. וַיַּכְּתוּם (Num. 14.45) is not derived from כָּתַת, 'but God knows best'. נַשַּׁנִי (Gen. 41. 51) is from נשש, because of the *dāgesh forte* in שׁ; were it from נשה the נ should either have *ḥīreq* with double שׁ or *qāmēṣ* without *dāgesh*. עִסּוּ (so, Ezek. 23. 3) he derives from עסס. Finally וְהַפִּתִּיתָ (Prov. 24. 28) from פתח is an irregular form.

Abul Walīd Ibn Janāḥ.

The progress made by Ḥayyūj's great discovery did not remain without consequences. His works were eagerly studied and scrutinized, and stimulated his fellow-workers to further efforts, and he has the undoubted merit of having paved the way for the compilation of the first complete Hebrew grammar. The man who could boast of this achievement was Abul Walīd Marwān b. Janāḥ (Jonah) of Cordoba. Born towards the end of the tenth century, he enjoyed for some time the tuition of Isaac b. Chiqatilla, one of the defenders of Menaḥem. His vocation in life was that of a physician. Inspired by Ḥayyūj's writings he devoted himself with intense zeal to the study of the Hebrew language. Later in life he was forced to leave Cordoba, and settled in Saragossa, where he died towards the middle of the eleventh century.

There is little doubt that his grammatical researches were furthered by Ḥayyūj's writings. He soon became aware that (as the instances given above show) many of the derivations taught by the latter were open to doubt, while a number of instances were overlooked by him altogether. He therefore compiled a supplementary treatise, which he entitled *Kitāb al-mustalḥaq.* The following is an extract from the preface to this work:

. . . For many years, while still in our country, I was engaged in supplementing what the illustrious Teacher and perfect Chief has omitted in his list of weak and double verbs . . . . He has overlooked many which he ought to have mentioned, and has omitted to explain forms obscure and difficult to understand. He has passed over various classes altogether, and forgotten a multitude of instances. I do not attach any blame to him for this, since human power is limited, perfection being God's alone. I am also in doubt concerning many questions in his two treatises, which I wish to clear up. This will be of considerable advantage, because these two classes of verbs form the most obscure chapters in the Hebrew language. Up till now I was debarred from this undertaking by the importance and overwhelming authority of this man who was neither preceded nor superseded by any one in his subject. We are, indeed, indebted to him for the boon he has conferred on us in elucidating obscure points and bringing near what was remote. Exile and travel connected therewith took my mind off the matter. A number of friends and lovers of research urged me to fulfil this task. In the following treatise I have endeavoured to *supplement*, to the best of my limited ability, the classes and individual forms which Abu Zakariyya has overlooked, and have called it *Al-mustalḥaq.*[1]

This work is of considerable length, surpassing in bulk Ḥayyūj's two treatises. The lists of the latter are enlarged by about fifty new roots. He also mentions a large number of others, to which he gives a different and more correct explanation. The work is of real scientific value, and reveals an astonishing mastery of the intricacies of the Hebrew irregular verbs. But the critic did not escape criticism. 'A gang of ignorant persons', jealous of the renown which the above-mentioned treatise had won for him, published an anonymous pamphlet blaming him for having omitted a number of verbs which, in their opinion, he should have included. This caused him to write a

[1] See Derenbourg, *Opuscules et Traités*, &c., Paris, 1880, p 248.

rejoinder, likewise in Arabic, under the title *Epistle of Admonition,*[1] in which he refutes the remarks of his opponents point by point. The bitterest sting is in the conclusion, in which he says that when their book, which had the title *Kitāb al-istīfā,*[2] became known, it was covered with such ridicule that its authors denied their authorship, and the book was named *Kitāb al-istikfā.*[3] In spite of its sarcastic tone this rejoinder enters deeply into the investigation of many irregular forms. A special feature of it is the occurrence of several quotations from ancient Arabic poets.

In order to realize how the spirit of the learned classes of Spanish Jewry was roused by Ibn Janāḥ's writings it is only necessary to bestow a glance at his next work, which is styled *Risālat al-taqrīb waltashīl,*[4] which is a kind of prolegomena to Ḥayyūj's treatises. It is introduced by a real or fictitious response to the demand of a friend who desired to have a vade-mecum for the inexperienced students of his earlier writings. It is given in the form of quotations from these books, with detailed comments attached to them. The *first* part is phonological, dealing with the vowels and quiescent letters. In the *second* part the author defends Ḥayyūj's denial of the existence of biliteral roots, while in the *third* he treats on the shortened imperfect and nouns derived from roots with a weak third radical. The discussion of roots with double consonants forms the conclusions.

The general flutter caused in the minds of his co-religionists is best illustrated by Abul Walīd's words prefacing another work which he published at that time:[5]

At a meeting with our dear friend Abū Suleimān Tarāqa we met a man who visits this neighbourhood. He thought that some people in his country objected to various points asserted by

[1] *Kitāb al-tanbīh,* ibid., p. 247.

[2] *The Satisfactory Book.*

[3] *At Hide and Seek.*

[4] *The Treatise of Bringing Near and Making Easy,* ibid., p. 268.

[5] Ibid., p. 344.

me in the *Mustalḥaq*, and intended to compile a book, had not God's goodness spared me. When I pressed him to declare himself explicitly he said that he only remembered a few words which he preferred to my opinion. When I demanded proofs in order to turn him away from his errors, he refused obstinately to listen. I saw that leaving the matter alone would be a shameful neglect for various reasons. One was that I could not allow these people to remain in their error, another that they would mislead other ignorant people who heard their words. The topic of the inflexion of verbs is very abstruse for intelligent people who have grown up in it, and much more so for such as form an opinion of it without any preliminary preparation to smooth the way for its comprehension. The mastery of this subject requires sound reasoning such as is granted only to few. Some people I cannot allow to judge my mind, although I do not imagine that I am free from imagination and proof against error. I was informed that he boasted to have conquered me at that meeting. Besides, I wished to retaliate and set his endeavour at nought, since he ventured on a branch of knowledge which he is unable to further, and approached a matter for which he was not prepared. This is the fruit of ignorance and the result of jealousy.

In the book itself, styled *Book of Reprisal*, the author describes the discussions he had with his interlocutor about a number of passages in the *Mustalḥaq*. In consequence of the obstinacy of the opponent the language is of unusual warmth, and expresses the author's indignation at being falsely accused of doing injustice to Ḥayyūj, of whom he was used to speak in terms of sincere admiration and respect. The book ends with the following characteristic line of poetry: 'If the scorpion turns back, we turn our back to it with the boot ready for it'. Far from being silenced, Ibn Janāḥ's opponents renewed their attacks, and they were now joined by the powerful statesman and scholar of no mean attainment, Samuel b. Nagdela.[1] The latter was no less an admirer of Ḥayyūj, yet he clung to the old

[1] See p 48.

theory of biliteral roots. In conjunction with Ibn Janāḥ's adversaries he launched a treatise against him under the title *Epistles of the Companions*,[1] of which unfortunately only a fragment containing the second chapter of the first part has come down to us. As it is limited to some details it is sufficient to reproduce the final words, which run as follows: 'As far as we are concerned we prefer the way of Abu Zakariyya, putting down his words and similar points, be they figurative or literal, but we find no pleasure in atrocity.'

Nothing daunted, Ibn Janāḥ immediately set to work to refute all his new opponents in a work which seems to have been of larger bulk, but of which only a small fragment has been saved. It is called *Kitāb al-tashwīr*,[2] and consists of four parts. The author himself quotes it frequently in his later works, and it is very probable that about the whole of it is embodied in them.

The researches preliminary to the composition of these five works naturally deepened Ibn Janāḥ's learning and ripened his judgement. We have his own words[3] that the last one in particular was very fruitful in giving him a clear insight into the working of the Hebrew language, so that he felt himself sufficiently prepared to undertake the compilation of his *magnum opus* which was to embrace a grammar as well as a lexicon. This he achieved in a work to which he gave the comprehensive title *Book of Detailed Investigation*. Both have fortunately been preserved in the Arabic originals as well as in the Hebrew translation by Judah b. Tabbon. The latter circumstance alone is sufficient to show the importance attached to it by the great masters of Hebrew learning in later generations. The grammar has a special title—*Book of coloured flower-beds*,[4] while the lexicon is simply styled *Book of Roots*, both forming a most imposing work.[5]

[1] *Rasāil al-rifāq*, see Derenbourg, ibid., pp. xlviii sqq. [2] Ibid., p. xlix.
[3] See *Riqmāh*, ed. Goldberg, p. xii. [4] *Kitāb al-luma'*, ed Lambert.
[5] *Kitāb al-uṣūl*, ed. Neubauer.

Why were nearly all the works mentioned hitherto written in Arabic? The answer is obvious. For Hebrew philology there was scarcely any other possibility on account of method and terminology, which at that time was firmly established in Arabic, but was in its infancy in Hebrew. This state of things is fuller illustrated in the preface of Ibn Janāḥ's book on grammar, of which I here give an abstract:

I have seen the people among whom we live making efforts to reach the utmost perfection in [the mastery of] their language, as appearance teaches and truth demands. The people of our tongue in the present generation have thrown this study behind their back, consider it superfluous and unworthy of attention. They thus miss the beauty of the language to such an extent that every one speaks according to his will, as if it were without system. They treat it, root and branch, with contempt, especially those who incline towards the study of the Talmud. I was told that one prominent talmudical scholar stated that there was no reason for the study of the language, that it was of no use, but vain trouble. Their reading of the Talmud itself is faulty to a degree, because they were not taught by competent persons. The consequence is that in their reading of the Bible they know no difference between the various vowels and accents. The knowledge of etymology and syntax they almost consider heresy. How different was this with the great Gaon Sa'adyāh, who devoted himself to the utmost of his ability to the study of the language, explaining its roots and the derivations therefrom in many of his books, especially in that known *Book of Languages*, as well as in other books. Also Samuel b. Hofni uttered grave warnings, supported by evidence, in praise of those who cared for the purity of the language . . .

Considering the prominent place occupied by linguistic research, we have resolved to compile a work comprising both the grammar with all its ways, and the roots which we find in the Bible, and explain them all. We will not leave unmentioned anything which may be of any use, to the best of our power My examples I intend to take as far as possible from the Bible, or, if not to be found there, from the Mishnāh or the Talmud, or from Aramaic, for this was the method adopted by Sa'adyāh in his treatise on the 'Seventy Words', as well as by Rabbi Sherirā, Rabbi Hāi, and others. If these should fail me I shall not hesitate to resort to Arabic, although some of my intelligent contemporaries forbear to do so. In this, too, I follow the example of Sa'adyāh, who often translates a strange word with an Arabic one of similar sound.[1] Our Rabbis also explained difficult words by similar ones in other languages . . .

The *Kitāb al-luma'* contains forty-six chapters, its arrangement being entirely in accordance with the standard Arabic works on grammar. It begins with the statement that the parts of speech in Hebrew, Arabic, and the cognate languages are *three*, viz. noun, verb, and particle. This is illustrated by numerous examples, showing at the same time how by a combination of these parts of speech sentences are formed. Later chapters deal with the classification of the consonants, composition of nouns, and their relation both to prefixes, suffixes, and prepositions. Other chapters deal with the interchange of consonants and the change of vowels, the formation of nouns with three or more consonants, the inflexion of the various classes of verbs, the pronouns, the copulative *wāw*, the construct state, plural forms, relative nouns, contractions, elliptic sentences, redundant constructions, repetitions, permutations, rare forms, transposition of letters, (*hysteron proteron*,) interrupted constructions, interrogation, statements, gender, and numeral.

We thus see that rules of phonology, accidence, and syntax are indissolubly mixed up exactly in the manner of Arab grammarians. This, however, has the advantage of introducing the student at once into the spirit of the language. Occasionally Arabic terminology is drawn upon. The following few specimens from the lexicon will suffice to illustrate his method.

דאה (Deut. 28. 49; Ps. 18. 11). The noun דאה (Lev. 11. 14) should by analogy be placed under the same root, originally דאיה.

[1] A well-known characteristic of Sa'adyāh.

This א is changed into י in הדיה (Deut. 14. 13 ; Isa. 34. 15) because the א is weak and assimilated to י, which therefore has *dāgesh forte.* The word designates a bird of prey.

חמאה. The א is omitted and its vowel given to the מ in חמה (Job 29. 6). In the plural מחמאות (Ps. 55. 22) the *pataḥ* under מ takes the place of *ṣērē*, and stands for מן חמאות.

חצן (Isa. 49. 22 ; Neh. 5. 13 ; Ps. 129. 7) means *forearm*, and is related to Arabic حضن (*bosom*), the part which is beneath the armpit and the waist. *Iḥtiḍān* means *carrying something in the bosom.* The woman carries (*iḥtăḍănăt*) her child, supporting it on her side.

מלתחה (2 Kings 10. 22), *keeper of clothes.* The word belongs to חתל (Ezek. 16. 4), but with transposition (of consonants). The word is also used for a *receptacle of garments*, as קמטריא in Targum, *qamtār* meaning a *box* in Arabic.

פזז (Gen. 49. 24 ; 2 Sam. 6. 16). The former quotation means *his arms were strong*, the latter *being alert, girded and resolute.* Related is מופז (1 Kings. 10. 18) and פז (Cant. 5. 11, &c.), both belonging to the same root. זהב מפז means the *best and purest gold*, while פז is the *noblest gold*, and the proof of it appears in another passage (2 Chron. 9. 17) viz. זהב טהור.

CHAPTER V

Samuel Nagdêla, Solomon Gebirol, Hāi Gaōn, Abul Faraj Hārūn, Abraham the Babylonian.

AMONG Ibn Janāḥ's opponents mentioned before there appeared the name of Samuel Nagdēla (Hannāgīd). His grammatical works, with the exception of some small fragments, are almost completely lost. They were written in Arabic under the title *Kitāb al-istighnā* (*Book of Amplitude*), and are probably identical with the 'Twenty-two treatises' mentioned by Ibn Ezra.[1] A number of quotations from this work is scattered in the biblical commentaries and grammatical writings of the latter. As to quotations from his works by Ibn Yashūsh, see below.

A small fragment from one of his treatises, probably the one just mentioned, has been discovered and published by Professor Kokovzov.[2] It is of lexicographical as well as exegetical character, alphabetically arranged, and must have been distinguished by great fullness. If all paragraphs of the book were discussed with the same amplitude the book must have been of considerable bulk. The fragment is unfortunately much broken, and no whole section can be extracted. He quotes Sa'adyāh, [Dūnāsh] b. Tamīm, Ibn Qoreish, and a certain Ibn Daniel, of whom nothing is known as yet. The following abstract is taken from the middle of the article on the root אמן:

ואהיה אצלו אמון (Prov. 8. 30) which he (Sa'adyāh) treats like המון, but this is remote. האמונים (Lam. 4. 5) *reared*, like אומן (Esther 2. 7). Ibn Qoreish explains נא אמון (Nahum 3. 8) as Alexandria, and אמון also *the high and noble one*, as in Exod. 17. 12,

[1] Cp. *Yesōd mōrā*, p. 5; cp. Derenbourg, ibid., p. 31.

[2] Ibid., pp. 205 sqq., and the fragment published Petrograd, 1905. *Acad.*, pp. 1366 sqq.

carried high, since he was weary with stretching them out humbly supplicating God. Similar תאמנה (Is. 60. 4) *they will be carried on the side.* נאמנים (Prov. 27. 6) *he feels safe from being hurt by the friend*; ויאמן (Exod. 4. 31) *the people believed*; נאמן (Isa. 22. 23, 25) *true*, as in Deut. 28. 59; Isa. 33. 16, *constant*; הָאֹמְנוֹת (2 Kings 18. 16) *pillars that carry*, as in Esther 2. 7. Ibn Daniel explains Exod. 17. 12, *lifted up*, and Hos. 5. 9 as Deut. 28. 59, *lasting*. Dūnāsh b. Tamīm explains אמן (Num. 5. 22; Neh. 8. 6) by *true*. The simple stem of the root also has the meaning of *fondling* in Esther 2. 7; 2 Kings 10. 1, with אחאב in the accusative. Further אומנת (Ruth 4. 16; 2 Sam. 4. 4). In passive, Lam. 4. 5, *brought up*, as אמונים (Ps. 12. 2 and 31. 24) *faithful*. The verbal noun occurs in באמנה (Esther 2. 20) like חֶטְאָה and שְׁגָגָה (Num. 15. 28)[1] . . .

[From the paragraph on אמץ]. אַמְצָה לִי (Zech. 12. 5) means *to be strong*, and then shall they *strengthen for me the inhabitants of Jerusalem and help them.* חזק ויאמץ (Ps. 27. 14), also תאמץ (Job 4. 4; Isa. 35. 3) *deliver them from their obligations.* אֲמֻצִּים Zech. 6. 3, 7, is explained as *painted red*, and Ibn Qoreish says it is like חמוץ בגדים (Isa. 63. 1) with change of ח and א, *red of cloth*, by which the prophet means the colour of vinegar. The Targum is קיטמין (*ashes*), גברא או כבדא. R. Sa'adyāh says *colour of ashes*, and the translation of ברדים אמצים with *black and white mixed* is admissible. R. Sa'adyāh on Prov. 24. 5[2] translates: 'O man [who is] wise with strength, and endowed with knowledge, and made vigorous with strength.'

SOLOMON B. GEBIROL.

The predominance of Arabic in works on the Hebrew language received a slight set back in a youthful contribution by Solomon b. Gebirol. This is a grammatical compendium in the shape of a Hebrew poem, which he states to have composed at the age of nineteen under the title of ענק (*Necklace*).[3] Only a fragment of it has been

[1] The text is much larger, but here interrupted by a gap.
[2] ed. Derenbourg, p. 134, with variations.
[3] ed. Senior Sachs and Egers, *Zunz Jubelschrift*, pp. 190 sqq.

preserved dealing mainly with phonological rules. The use of Hebrew was probably dictated by the poetic form.

'Solomon, the Spaniard', he says in the Introduction, 'made a compendium of the holy language for the scattered nation. My heart pondered over the community of the Rock, and examined their small remnant. Then I saw that the holy tongue was gone from them, and has disappeared almost entirely. Their speech is un-Hebrew, and one would not recognize the language of Judah. One half of them speaks Edomite (Spanish), and the other Arabic . . . . I considered in my heart to write a book on the elements of the grammar of the holy tongue . . . . I wrote it in rhymed verse for remembering it better, and divided it into ten parts . . . and called it *'Anāq*'.

Hāi Gaon.

At about the same time when Ibn Janāḥ wrote his great dictionary, the Gaon Hāi in Babylonia was engaged in the authorship of a similar work, likewise written in Arabic, and published under the title *al-hāwi* (the *collecting* one). The book was superseded in the west by Ibn Janāḥ's labours, and in the east by those of Abul Faraj Harūn (see below), and is now known only by a few quotations in Judah b. Bal'am's writings. It was arranged in alphabetical order according to the last letter of roots, in accordance with the custom of Arab lexicographers.

ABUL FARAJ HĀRŪN.

In the year 1028 Abul Faraj, 'the Anonymous Grammarian of Jerusalem', as Ibn Ezra calls him, finished a large work styled *The Comprehensive Book on the Roots and Branches of the Hebrew Language.*[1] It consists of *eight* sections, the first six dealing with grammar. The *seventh* section forms a dictionary, while the last one treats on the Aramaic portions of the Bible. The language of the work is Arabic. As Ḥayyūj's writings had remained unknown

[1] See Bacher, *RÉJ.*, vol. 30.

to him, he was still in the ban of the older views, and therefore divided the letters of the alphabet into two groups, just as his predecessors did. In the arrangement of his dictionary he adopted a new method. He takes a triliteral root and discusses its various meanings and applications. He then rearranges the order of the consonants, and discourses on the new roots evolving from the change in the same way, e.g. קרב, קבר; ברק, בקר; רבק, רקב. The following is a specimen:

צֶלַע in this order of consonants yields the following meanings: (1) *rib* (Gen. 2. 21); (2) *side* (Exod. 26. 20, 26, 27, 35); *side of a mountain* (2 Sam. 16. 13); (3) *side wing of the Temple* (Ezek. 41. 6), which is also explained as *windows*; (4) *name of a place* (Joshua 18. 28; 2 Sam. 21. 14); (5) *to limp* (Gen. 32. 32; Ps. 35. 15; Jer. 20. 10). If the letters be rearranged in the order עָלַץ they give the meaning of *rejoicing* (1 Sam. 2. 1; Prov. 11. 10; Hab. 3. 14; Ps. 25. 2). In the order עָצֵל the root means *to be idle* (Prov. 19. 24, 15; 26. 13; 31, 27; Eccles. 10. 18).

From the concluding chapter on Biblical Chaldee:[1]

The Hebrew language does not afford us any claim to the knowledge of Chaldee as regards the tenses, the inflexion of the verb, and the declension of the noun, the difference between the absolute and construct state, or what is connected and disconnected, or any other matters which we are able to establish firmly in Hebrew. Chaldee is not our language, and what is extant of it is not nearly as much (as in Hebrew). The results to be gained from its exposition are only proportionate. Moreover, all we know of its ways does not move in one direction, as is the case in Hebrew, in which fixed forms, correct analogies, the relation of parallel forms to one another, the use of homonyms, and the reduction of rare forms to such as are well established, as well as the explanation of anomalies not settled by exceptionless rules are general. The cognizance of the character of this language is obtainable by various means; e.g. in some instances the past tense in Chaldee is like the imperative in Hebrew. This is

[1] See my *Arabic Chrestomathy in Hebrew Characters*, p. 54.

particularly the case with the triliteral verb. Thus אזל (Dan. 2. 17, 24) is in both instances past tense, meaning *he went*, which is like the verbal noun[1] of the same verb (1 Sam. 9. 7; Job 14. 11) in Hebrew, according to the requirements of the form. Likewise קצף (Dan. 2. 12) is past tense, and would in Hebrew correspond to an imperative קְצַף if that were possible, like שְׁכַב, were not the imperfect וַיִּקְצֹף (Exod. 16. 20) . . .

This chapter establishes Harūn's claim to be the first to have attempted, though crudely, a grammar of the Aramaic portions of the Bible.

Apart from this *Comprehensive* work, Hārūn composed another, which, according to its title *Al-kāfi* (*The Adequate One*), seems to have served as a supplement to the former. This may be gathered from a remark by the author in a fragment, probably of his *Comment on Words*,[2] in which both works are mentioned together. Now although the *Kāfi* is apparently lost, the author has left two compendia, part of one of which is extant among the Genizah fragments in the British Museum. This is styled *Kitāb al-ʿuqūd* (*Book of Pearl Strings*) *on the inflexion of the Hebrew language*).[3] Of the earlier compendium no trace is at present known, but the author alludes to it in the preface to the other in the following words: 'I made an abridgement of the *Kāfi* which comprehends all its chapters except those dealing with anomalous forms, and apart from the additions contained in the *Kāfi*. I was asked to compile another compendium more concise than the one mentioned, binding together the rules of inflexion in a comprehensive manner. Some of these are fundamental, and can be mastered in a very short time. I am endeavouring to produce this compendium, which, if omitted, would not matter much, but I will enlarge upon a subject which deserves to be begun, asking God to save me from mistakes

[1] The Arabic *al amr* is generally used for the *imperative*. This form does not occur in the Hebrew Bible, but in Aramaic (Ezra 5. 15) it is אֱזֵל.

[2] Cf. Poznański, *RÉJ.*, 33, p. 214.

[3] See my publication in *J.Q.R.*, N.S. xiii, pp. 1 sqq.

in His kindness and mercy. The knowledge of the Hebrew language is required on account of the obligation to be familiar with the exact explanation of the divine law, but this cannot be gained by him whose duty it is (to do so) as long as he is ignorant of the language, because of the errors he will commit.'

The Qaraite point of view of the author is clearly brought out in the concluding words.

ABRAHAM THE BABYLONIAN.

With the decline of the literary life among the Jews of Babylon their linguistic pursuits began to wane. During this period we only hear of one more name, viz. that of ABRAHAM THE BABYLONIAN. His contribution to Hebrew linguistics has only an historical interest, as he still clung to the primitive theory of monoliteral roots. He left a small treatise of lexicographical character, of which only a fragment has been preserved,[1] the last remnant of a system which had lost force both in east and west.

The work consists of five divisions: (1) roots of one to four letters; (2) cognate roots of the same consonants, but changing their positions; (3) roots of identical consonants but of different meanings; (4) roots which require to be supplemented by another consonant; (5) roots with consonants which permit interchange with cognate ones. The greatest originality is displayed in group 4, which contains items quite in harmony with modern criticism, and of which the following is a specimen in concise form. Many are of surprising ingenuity:

אח (Ezek. 18. 10) stands for אחת; דל (Ps. 141. 3) for דלת; הבכא (Ps. 84. 7) for הברכה; ללת (1 Sam. 4. 19) for ללדת; יהל (Isa. 13. 20) for יאהל; יהל אור (Job 31. 26) for יהלו אורם; ויגש שאול (1 Sam. 9. 18) for ויפגש; וירב בנחל (1 Sam. 15. 5) for ויארב בנחל; גא מאד (Isa. 16. 6) for גאה; בלבת אש (Exod. 3. 2) for בלהבת; צר ואור (Isa. 5. 30) for יצהר; וירפו (2 Kings 2. 22) for

[1] See Neubauer, *Jrn. As.*, 1863, II, pp. 195 sqq.

וירפאו; כלו בבית (1 Sam. 6. 10) for כלאו; תוי (Job 31. 35) for תתאו; הליכי בחמה (Job 29. 6) for בחמאה; ותזרני (2 Sam. 22. 40) for ותאזרני; רמים (Ps. 22. 22) for ראמים; בנו (1 Sam. 25. 8) for באנו; סותה (Gen. 49. 11) for כסותו; לביא (Jer. 39. 7 and 2 Chr. 31. 10) for להביא; קט (Ezek. 16. 47) for קטן; ועלתה כאור (Amos 8. 8) for כיאור; מכלת (1 Kings 5. 25) for מאכלת; שֵׁרית (1 Chron. 12. 39) for שארית; שלתך (1 Sam. 1. 17) for שאלתך; שקר מזין (Prov. 17. 4) for מאזין; לרום (Ezek. 46. 14) for לערום.

CHAPTER VI

Moses b. Samuel b. Chiqatilla, Isaac b. Yashūsh, Judah b. Bal'am, Isaac b. Barūn, Judah Hallevi.

UP to this time, the beginning of the twelfth century, linguistic research kept within the bounds of Arabic speech, and was therefore withheld from perusal by the Jews of Europe outside Spain. So it came about that even Rashi remained unacquainted with the whole later developments, and could only satisfy his undoubted philological bent by relying on Menaḥem, who had long been superseded by the school of Ḥayyūj and Ibn Janāḥ. The want of translations made itself felt. The first of these was provided by MOSES B. SAMUEL B. CHIQATILLA of Cordoba, a contemporary of Rashi. He was a prolific Bible exegete, and the first who applied the grammatical results of the two authorities just named. His exegetical writings have unfortunately been lost, except a number of fragments preserved in the shape of quotations in the works of later commentators.[1] Many of his comments, of which the following is a specimen, are of grammatical character:

מוסד מוּסָּד (Isa. 28. 16). The former is participle passive, the latter a verbal noun, while the *dāgesh forte* in ס is not of the same nature as in יִסַּדְתָּ, which denotes the *Pi'ēl*, as in דִּבַּרְתָּ or אִבַּדְתָּ (Ps. 9. 6). The *dāgesh forte* in מוּסָּד serves to mark the assimilation of the first radical in Qal. The noun is מיסד in a form like מִבְטָח (Ps. 65. 6), but not participle Hoph'al, as Ibn Janāḥ assumes, because Hoph'al belongs to Hiph'il, as Mephu'āl to Pi'ēl. There is a difference between צְבִי מֻדָּח (Isa. 13. 14) and מְנֻדָּח (Isa. 8. 22), because the former belongs to the Hiph'il class, as מוּשְׁלָח, while מְנֻדָּח is a Pu'al form like מְדוּבָּר.

[1] See Poznański, *Ibn Chiquitilla nebst den Fragmenten seiner Schriften* (1895), p. 100.

Note this well; and since we do not find an imperative form of מוסר, viz. הוֹסִיד or הוֹסֵד, I do not put it to Hiph'il. The first (מוסר) may be מֵיְסִיד like משמין, but not מִשְׁמַן (Ps. 78. 31), because the *shūreq* is like ḥōlem, and מוסר like מוֹדַע, and not participle passive.

Moses Chiqatilla's bent for grammatical pursuits found a more important outlet in his translation of Ibn Ḥayyūj's epoch-making treatises on the weak roots and those with double letters.[1] As he states in the preface to this work, he undertook it at the behest of a certain Isaac Hanna'īm b. Solomon Hannāsi, which shows that the desire to have these books at the disposal of students must have become widespread. The great fame which Ḥayyūj's work had attained is further evidenced by the fact that a grammarian of the calibre of Abraham b. Ezra produced another Hebrew translation.[2] What induced him to do so is not clear. It was probably the circumstance that Moses Chiqatilla adorned his translation with additions and annotations. There is also a difference in the terminology of both translators.

Not satisfied with merely reproducing another's work, Moses Chiqatilla compiled an independent treatise on the *Masculine and Feminine Genders*, written in Arabic. The bulk of the work is unfortunately lost, but a few leaves have been saved, and are extant among the Genizah collections of Cambridge and the British Museum.[3] Both fragments belonged to the same volume, and are, as G. Margoliouth has pointed out, in autograph, and probably the first rough draft containing corrections and omissions. These fragments evidently belonged to an earlier part of the work, because they are principally introductory. A number of fragments exist in Leningrad, and have been

[1] Cp. Ewald and Dukes, *Beiträge*, &c. (1844).

[2] Nutt, *Two Treatises* (1870).

[3] Those of the latter were published by G. Margoliouth in *JQR.*, 1902, pp. 312 sqq. For a second fragment see Appendix II, and for a third, Kokovzov, ibid., pp. 59–66.

published by Professor Kokovzov in the volume mentioned before. We learn from it that the material of the work was arranged alphabetically, as the following abstract shows:[1]

אַיָּלָה שְׁלֻחָה (Gen. 49. 21) is a *nomen speciei*; the plural of אַיָּל is אַיָּלִים (Lam. 1. 6), but אַיִל is in plural אֵילִים (Num. 7. 17) especially in connexion with צאן, which has no feminine form.

אֵלָה is the name of the oak, also generalized as in Ezek. 6. 13. It has a plural masculine in Isa. 1. 29, and feminine אֵילוֹת (1 Kings 9. 26), applied to the frequency of the trees in this place.

אכף is of the same form as ארץ, with suffix in Job 33. 7, like אַרְצִי.

אֲלֻמָּה-אלמה (Gen. 37. 7); the plural is masculine אֲלֻמִּים (ibid.), but feminine אֲלֻמֹּתֵיכֶם (ibid.).

אלף numeral masc. gen. (Exod. 38. 26, &c.), up to *ten* and further to תשעה עשר אלף, masc.

אֵם *mother*, fem. gen. with suffix אמי, &c., but not אמתי; in plural לְאִמֹּתָם (Lam. 2. 12).

אָמָה *handmaid*, originally אמהה, with one ה which is the third radical omitted, while the ה showing the feminine termination remains. When contracted the ה reappears as in הָאֲמָהוֹת (2 Sam. 6. 22), and in construct state אַמְהוֹת (ibid. 20).

אום *nation*, plur. אֻמִּים (Ps. 117. 1); *fem. gen.* אֻמּוֹת (Num. 25. 15). The plural of אֵימָה is אֵימִים (Job 20. 25), *masc. gen.*, and אימות, *fem.* (Ps. 55. 5).

ISAAC B. YASHŪSH.

Isaac (Abu Ibrahīm) b. Yashūsh was a native of Toledo, where he died in 1057 at the age of seventy-five.[2] His contributions to grammatical studies consisted of a treatise on *Conjugations*, likewise written in Arabic. This work also is lost with the exception of a few fragments, of which several specimens were published with French translation by the late Professor J. Derenbourg. The composition of this book seems to have been prompted by the writings of Ibn Janāḥ

[1] pp. 59 sqq.

[2] See Derenbourg, *Opuscules*, p. 20.

and Samuel Hannāgīd, who were his contemporaries. The latter of the two is mentioned in the work as defunct. The following is a brief extract:[1]

The Nāgīd (of blessed memory) is of opinion that the last radical in עשה, קנה, בנה, &c., is י. On this question he differs from all other authorities, considering these roots to be עשי, בני, קני, &c., and supports his theory by forms like נִטָּיוּ (Num. 24. 6; Ps. 73. 2), חָסָיוּ (Deut. 32. 37), יִשְׁלָיוּ (Job 12. 6), יִרְבְּיֻן (Deut. 8. 13), יִבְכָּיוּן (Isa. 33. 7), &c., as well as פִּדְיוֹן, עליון, כליון (Isa. 10. 22), פדיון, and similar ones, in which the final radical י has been replaced by ה, the real radical י, &c.

If anything this specimen shows how strongly the study of Hebrew was fertilized by being grafted with an Arabic scion.

Judah b. Bal'am.

The new centre for the study of Hebrew, begun in Toledo, produced another teacher more distinguished than the one just mentioned. His name was Judah b. Bal'am. He was not only a biblical scholar of high rank, but an original thinker in matters grammatical. Of his personal affairs nothing is known except that he was a lover of Arabic literature, prose as well as poetry. In his biblical commentaries, written in Arabic, he allowed full play to his grammatical propensities, as the following specimen shows:[2]

(Isa. 8. 11). In וְיִסְּרֵנִי the ר should have *pataḥ* instead of *ṣērēh*, because the verb is the past tense of Pi'ēl. I maintain that this instance as well as similar ones are in the past tense, although the preceding י would let it appear as future tense, because I well consider the root. The element which alters the past for future, viz. the ו, is a mere addition. If it be omitted the past would stand. If in ויעשו, ויראו, ויבנו the *pataḥ* of the י be added to future forms, the same rule would be in force because the ו that turns the future into past is likewise a (mere) addition, while the forms themselves are future.

[1] See Derenbourg, *Opuscules*, p. 20.

[2] Cp. *RÉJ.*, 23, p. 225.

(Isa. 64. 5) וַנָּבֶל. Abul Walīd says that the radical נ is omitted from a form וננבל, as in כִּנְבֹל (Isa. 34. 4). Another opinion is that the נ of the future tense has been dropped. In any case the root is נבל. Whoever derives the word from a different root which does not possess this meaning, and compares it with וַנָּשֶׁב (Gen. 43. 21) errs greatly. This is utterly remote: heaven forbid that I should be entangled in such bad work.

Judah b. Bal'am's acquaintance with Arabic literature in connexion with his tendency to specialize, led him to introduce a new element into Hebrew rhetoric not thought of by any of his predecessors. This is the *tajnīs*.[1] The nearest translation of this term is paronomasia,[2] although it is not exactly the same on account of the absence of vowels. In Hebrew and Arabic it describes words of identical consonantic spelling which allows wide differences of reading. The work has come down to us in incomplete form. The same is the case with the Hebrew version by an unknown translator. Both were published side by side by Professor Kokovzov in the volume mentioned before.[3] The following specimens are taken from the Arabic original:

דרור דרור. *First* (Lev. 25. 10) meaning *freedom*. It is also applied to the fragrance and purity of musk, as in Exod. 30. 23. *Second* (Ps. 84. 4), the name of a clean bird. Abul Walīd thinks it to be a clean bird, taking his proof from the words *thy altars*, but this is not plausible, because the words *thy altars* refers back to v. 3. My explanation of this passage is that *my soul yearns to abide in the strongholds of my Lord*, and to utter praise at His altars. V. 4 (a) stands between the two passages. The meaning is that the bird occupies a nest where he can put his fledgeling in safety. I, however, find no rest, but am always roaming about. This he (David) said without doubt at the time of his flight from before Saul.

מדבר מדבר. The first as in Exod. 19. 1, and well known; the second Cant. 4. 3, *speech*.

[1] Cp. *JQR.*, 10, p. 397; Steinschneider, *Ar. Lit. d. J.*, p. 139; Mehren, *Rhetorik der Araber*, p. 154.

[2] Inadequately described by Bacher, p. 60; see also Dukes in *Litbl. d. P.*, 9, p. 453.

[3] pp. 67 sqq. (Texts).

דל דל. The first, *poor*, Exod. 23. 3, and from this *sick*, as in 2 Sam. 13. 4 and Ps. 41. 2; second, Ps. 141. 3, referring to *speech*, as in Zech. 9. 1, an oracle, although the meaning (of משא) is *lifting up*. The explanation, *weakness of my lips*, is inadmissible, because one would not pray to guard the weakness of lips.

Another proof of our author's propensity to specialize is his essay on the Hebrew particles, or what he considered as such. Like his other works it was written in Arabic, but has till lately been known only in Hebrew translation.[1] Thanks to Kokovzov's labours we are now in the possession of some specimens of the original.[2] It consists of a reasoned list of the items in alphabetical order, explaining each in various shades of meaning to suit the context as well as its grammatical application, occasionally even in comparison with Aramaic parallels. The treatise embraces a number of words which are really nouns, but are treated adverbially. As the Hebrew version exists in print there is no need to insert any specimen here.

Of special interest is another treatise by Judah b. Bal'am, in which he gives evidence of acute power of observation. He is the first Jewish linguist who discusses the denominative verb, or verbal forms which take their origin not from a verbal root, but from nouns. This phenomenon can be observed in every language. In a brief prefatory remark he states that he has followed Arabic usage. Like the rest of his treatises this one is written in Arabic, of which fragments are to be found in Kokovzov's publication.[3] A Hebrew translation has been known for some time.[4] The paragraphs are arranged in alphabetical order. It is one of the most interesting of his works, although modern lexicography would not agree with various of his deductions. Besides, he by no means exhausted the subject. This could hardly be expected, as it requires the profoundest scrutiny. One small specimen will suffice to illustrate the author's methods:

[1] החקר, vol. I.
[2] Ibid., pp. 109 sqq.
[3] Ibid., pp. 133 sqq.
[4] ed. Pollack in הכרמל, 3, pp. 213 sqq.

ברך 2 Chron. 6. 13; Gen. 24. 11; 41. 43 (אברך). All these instances are taken from the derived stem (Aph'el) and from בִּרְכַּיִם. As to Gen. 24. 11 it is known that he (Eliezer) made the camels lie down on their haunches. אַבְרֵךְ is an infinitive as אַשְׁכֵּם (so Jer. 25. 3), while the א stands for ה. I translate it in the sense of humility, viz. 'bow down to people'.

There is another work attributed to Judah b. Bal'am, but its authenticity has not been established beyond doubt. It is of masoretic character, and bears the title טעמי המקרא [1] Whether it was written in Hebrew or Arabic is likewise uncertain. The work was edited by John Mercer, Paris, 1566, and is now very rare. An appendix to this volume treats on the accents of the Books of Psalms, Proverbs, and Job. The authenticity of the latter, which was written in Arabic, has been impugned with strong reasons, although its original language brings it into line with all the other works of Ibn Bal'am. As the extant manuscripts of the original describe it as a compendium, we might assume that it is an abridgement of a larger work originally styled *Guide of the Reader*. This was undoubtedly written in Arabic, and *perhaps* by Ibn Bal'am,[2] but the question must remain open till more reliable information is forthcoming.

Isaac b. Barūn.

On the authority of Ibn Ezra,[3] the names of two authors, of whose works only the titles are at present known, must be mentioned here. The one is David b. Ḥajar of Granada, who composed a treatise on *The Kings*, probably of masoretic character, and dealing with a certain class of accents. The other is Levi (Abulfăhm) b. Al Tabbān of Saragossa, author of a work styled *The Key*.[4] More

[1] Cp. Wickes, טעמי אמ"ת, Oxford, 1881, p. 106.

[2] Wickes, p. 104, denies this, but the words זיאדה ללמעלם סעיד עלי צאחב אלכתאב does not point to a certain סעיד as the author, but perhaps annotator.

[3] See Bacher, *Ibn Ezra als Grammatiker*, p. 185.

[4] המפתח.

fortunate than the latter was his disciple ISAAC B. BARŪN.[1] In his work *Comparison between the Hebrew and Arabic Languages* he took up the work of the most eminent of his predecessors, notably Ibn Qoreish and Judah b. Bal'am. Ibn Barūn's treatise is likewise written in Arabic. It consists of two parts, the shorter being grammatical, the longer lexicographical. He was so well trained in Arabic literature that his paragraphs are studded with quotations from the Diwāns of Arabic poets. Of particular interest are the points of contact he has with Judah b. Bal'am's treatise on the denominative verb, but it does not appear that he had any cognizance of the existence of this treatise, although he quotes his name in other connexions. What is at present known of the relics of his writings is supplemented by the reproduction of fragments in Professor Kokovzov's volume.[2] The following specimens will illustrate his method as well as his critical powers, and may even be regarded as contributions to the Arabic dictionary:

אתון (*she ass*) is the same form as *atān* in Arabic. איתן (Num. 24. 21) is in my opinion closely related to *ātān*, meaning a moss-covered rock in the water, which is therefore very dangerous. The poet sings:[3] '[I swear] by a rock which I once saw descending into the water, and it does not taste moisture.' This translation is supported by the word 'rock' in the second half of the verse, being an allusion to the firmness of rocks. Similar is Mic. 6. 2, speaking of mountains, as shown by 'mountains' in the same verse. Abul Walīd places איתן under the root אית, treating the נ as added. I do not know what made him do it We do not find any evidence of it. Additional is the י rather than the נ. The form is necessarily the same as אסין, concerning which he (Abul Walīd) states that, since it offers no etymological proof of being derived from a root with a weak third radical, he is of opinion that the נ is a radical letter and cannot be treated as added without proof. This he says in the paragraph on אסן.

[1] Cp. Neubauer, ibid., p. 204; Derenbourg, *Opuscules*, p. xx; Bacher.
[2] Ibid., pp. 153 (Texts) sqq.
[3] Name of poet and place of the verse at present unknown.

I should like to know what proof or argument or etymology is found for איתן which would make the י radical and the נ additional.

בלת (Job 14. 12). For this word I find affiliation to Arabic בלת, meaning *to sever, to cut.* The meaning of the above quotation is: *till the heavens are severed.* The same meaning appertains to Num. 14. 16, i.e. *the power of God be cut?* Likewise Isa. 10. 25.

בסר (Jer. 31. 30), identical with Arabic בֻּסֿר, meaning *unripe dates,* sing. בֻּסֿרה, only 'with us' the word is applied to every unripe fruit.

גרזן, related to אלכרזן, a large axe with which the tree is cut. It is said (proverbially): 'An axe that has no edge is like a stick.'

תהו (Gen. 1. 2), in Arabic ארץ תִּיהָא, *desert land,* where neither a road nor help is found, as in Isa. 45. 18, which means: 'I have created it for habitation, but not that it should be desert land'. One says (in Arabic) ארץ תיה ותיהא. See also Isa. 29. 21. As to Isa. 24. 10, it means: *city of bewilderment,* i.e. amazing greatness. This is also expressed in the root תאה. A support for this explanation is given in the previous description of the city (Tyre) in Isa. 23. 8 and 22. 2.

Judah Hallevi.

A striking feature of the works of the older grammarians is the large space given to phonology. This is quite natural in view of the phenomena and rules of this part of Hebrew grammar, which is incomparably more expansive and complicated than in Arabic. This complication and the uncertainties springing therefrom are fully reflected in modern works on Hebrew grammar, and it is no wonder that they are not satisfactorily removed by the medieval Jewish authors. This state of things is well illustrated in the remarks of Judah Hallevi, who discoursed on this subject in the famous *Kitāb al-khazari.*[1] He advanced some original ideas concerning the relation of Hebrew to Aramaic and Arabic. 'Abraham,' he says, 'who was an Aramaean

[1] II, 80; see my edition, pp. 131 sqq.

by birth, employed his native tongue for daily use only, but Hebrew as a holy language. Ishmael brought it to the Arabic-speaking nations, which accounts for the similarity between these languages.' Like most educated Jews in Spain he was versed in Arabic poetry, but he recognized that the forms of Arabic prosody could only be adapted to Hebrew verse with the sacrifice of several fundamental rules of Hebrew phonology. He perceived that the nature of the short syllable in Hebrew was not suited to Arabic prosody, and that Hebrew poets did violence to the language by dividing or closing open syllables and opening closed ones.[1] It is curious that Judah Hallevi is himself frequently guilty of the same practice, but he saw the impossibility of adopting the Arabic form of verse-making. 'He who intends to do this (viz. write on the accents) must omit poetry, because it can only be recited in one way. For it mostly joins where it should be disjunctive, and stops where it should go on' (II. 72). In his discussion of the vowels, Judah Hallevi starts from the three fundamental vowels *u*-, *a*-, *i*-, as in Arabic. It is peculiar that he places both kinds of *qāmeṣ* into the first class, making it appear as though he pronounced the ordinary long *qāmeṣ*, like the *a* in *water*. In the classification of the Hebrew nouns he distinguishes three forms, viz. (1) the ordinary etymological formation; (2) changes produced by the rules of syntax; (3) changes caused by accents A discussion of the accents concludes his brief survey of this chapter of Hebrew grammar.

[1] See above, p. 26.

CHAPTER VII

The school of Rashi, Nathan b. Jeḥiel, Menaḥem b. Solomon, Nathanael.

However great was the progress that had been made up to the end of the eleventh century in Hebrew grammar and lexicography, the results were accessible only to those who had mastered the Arabic language. The Jews in Christian Spain, France, Germany, and Italy were, with few exceptions, debarred from using the 'external' literature then available. Glaring instances of this disadvantage are patent in the country of Rashi and his two grandsons, Samuel b. Meir and Jacob Tam. For their lexicographical studies they all relied on Menaḥem's dictionary, but with the criticisms and supplements by Dūnāsh and his supporters. Rashi, however, did not follow Menaḥem blindly, but showed by his remarks that, without being acquainted with Ḥayyūj's discovery, he seems to have entertained some half correct notions with regard to triliteral roots. This is aptly illustrated by the following specimen from his commentary on the Pentateuch:

ונצלתם (Exod. 3. 22). Onqelos translates *you will render Egypt empty*, see 12. 36; 33. 6, the נ being a radical letter. Menaḥem in his *Machbereth* holds צ to be the first letter, quoting Gen. 31. 9, 16. His words are not, however, correct, for had not the נ been radical, while having *ḥireq*, the form would not have been active, but passive as in ונסחתם (Deut. 28. 63; Lev. 26. 25; Ezek. 22. 21; Jer. 7. 10). Every נ, which sometimes is written and at other times missing, as in נוגף, נושא, נותן, נושך (in participle Qal) has *Sh*ᵉ*wā mobile* in the second person plural of the past tense as in וּנְשָׂאתֶם (Gen. 45. 19; Num. 32. 29; Gen. 17. 11).[1]

[1] Rashi derives ונמלתם from נמל.

I say, therefore, that this letter with *ḥireq* is radical, the form being a *Pi'ēl*, *as* דִּבּוּר, כִּפּוּר, לִמּוּד, in which instances the first radical has *ḥireq*, as in ודברתם (Num. 20. 8 ; Ezek. 45. 20 ; Deut. 11. 19).

Jacob Tam was even more conservative, and took up the cudgels on behalf of Menaḥem against Dūnāsh. His imperfect preparation for this undertaking he endeavoured to make good by a close acquaintance with Hebrew, feeling his way by intuition rather than by the help of the rules of grammar. Yet he so far felt the necessity of systematizing the Hebrew vocabulary that he arranged the whole of it in twelve classes. In the *first* section he placed biliteral roots ; *second*, hollow roots ; *third*, verba ל"ה ; *fourth*, verba פ"ן ; *fifth*, פ"י ; *sixth*, פ"י and ל"ה ; *seventh*, פ"ן and ל"ה ; *eighth*, ע"ע : *ninth*, forms like נָמוֹג ; *tenth*, forms like דומם ; *eleventh*, ordinary three radical roots ; *twelfth*, stems with more than three radicals.[1]

It is easily seen that the number *twelve* is artificial, and one cannot avoid the suspicion that in conformity with the spirit of the age some astrological influence was at work in bringing up the number of verbal classes to that of the signs of the zodiac. Of no more than literary interest is Jacob Tam's poem on the accents.[2]

Much superior in his attainments as Hebrew linguist was Jacob's elder brother Samuel (commonly known as Rashbam), whose commentary on the Pentateuch is studded with a large number of grammatical observations. He operates with triliteral roots, although he does not seem to have read Ḥayyūj's treatises. Ample evidence of this is given in his explanations of irregular verbal forms the roots of which are not conspicuous at a glance. An instance of his advance beyond Menaḥem is given in his note on Exod. 18. 9,[3] where he, in contrast to the latter, recognized the real root of the verb in question. The following specimen shows a divergence between him and his grand-

[1] See Dunāsh, loc. cit., p. 38 (הכרעות).

[2] See Halberstamm in Kobak's ישורון, 5, p. 123.

[3] וַיִּחַדְּ.

father Rashi, but to the advantage of the latter, whose explanation is shared by modern scholars:

והמם (Deut. 7. 23) is explicitly like סבב and שמם (Lam. 5. 18) with double מ. The meaning of the verse is this: He made the noise of great tumult and thunder in battle till they were destroyed. If the second מ were suffix the word would have been וְהֲמָמָם,[1] and were the root המה it would be וְהָמָם, like עָשָׂם (Isa. 48. 5), and רָאָם (Gen. 32. 3). וְהָמָם cannot be explained in the same way, because הָמוֹן expresses physical emotion, as does יֶהֱמֶה (Jer. 48. 36, cp. Ps. 46. 4). Had the Prophet intended to use the transitive form, he would have said וְהַמָּם (with *dāgesh forte*) as in Lam. 2. 22; 4. 11; 2 Kings 25. 29; Isa. 28. 28.

Nathan b. Jeḥiel.

At the turn of the twelfth century the Jews of Italy made a belated entry into the field of Hebrew linguistics, not, indeed, with the endeavour of carrying its study further, but in order to render the mass of rabbinic writings accessible to people who lacked the traditional interpretation of the older authorities. This task was undertaken by Nathan b. Jeḥiel, of Rome, who died at the beginning of the twelfth century. He is the author of the famous *Ārūkh*, a comprehensive dictionary of the Talmud, the Targums, and the Midrashim. The accomplishment of so gigantic a work will always command the admiration of students, for many reasons. To procure the bare literary material must have entailed great difficulty and labour, not to speak of the much enlarged linguistic compass of post-biblical writings presenting a vocabulary swelled by a variety of dialects, foreign words, new forms. The author had to open up new paths in a work that covers an enormous ground. Many definite results cannot, of course, be expected with so huge a subject-matter, especially as Nathan, being unacquainted with the labours of the Spanish school, moved within the confines of the grammatical

[1] Rashi says distinctly that the second מ is not a radical.

notions of Menaḥem. The work is also important in another direction, inasmuch as it has preserved a large number of correct readings from old manuscripts. Not less momentous was the impulse it gave to subsequent lexicographers, an impulse which has maintained its force almost down to our days. Its popularity became speedily so great that it was frequently copied, and many manuscripts of it are extant. The first edition formed one of the earliest products of the printing press, probably before 1480. Edition followed edition. In 1655 Benjamin Musaphia, of Amsterdam, re-edited the work with many additions and corrections under the title מוסף הערוך. Prior to this Menaḥem di Lonzano supplemented the *Ārūkh* by notes on the foreign words occurring in the Talmud.[1] Abridged editions were printed as early as 1511, and successively several times.[2] The enlarged editions of modern times are outside the scope of this treatise.

Menaḥem b. Solomon.

What slow progress Ḥayyūj's discovery made in Italy is further illustrated by a new work from the hand of Nathan's compatriot Menaḥem b. Solomon, of Rome, who in 1142 completed a dictionary of Biblical Hebrew under the title *Ebhen Bōḥan* ('Touchstone'), in which he endeavoured to supplement several omissions in the *Ārūkh*. Of real criticism the work offers little, because the author merely corrects several errors in Menaḥem b. Saruk's explanations, again ignoring Ḥayyūj's and Ibn Janāḥ' writings. Merely as a literary curiosity I insert a brief specimen :[3]

בן sometimes expresses the idea of guilt, e.g. 1 Sam. 20. 31; 25. 17; Deut. 25. 2. Although in the last-named instance ב has

[1] See המעריך, ed. Jellinek, 1853; cf. David Cohen de Lara.

[2] Cracow, 1511 and 1592; Prague, 1707, 1863.

[3] See Bacher in the Graetz *Jubelschrift*, p. 94.

ḥīreq, it also means being guilty of wickedness. In 1 Sam. 18. 17 it means worthy of being chief of the army. In Isaiah 21. 10 the rebellious community is compared to the corn that is threshed in the barn and to the nail fastened in the midst of the threshing-floor on which the rope is fastened. The other end of the rope is tied to the horn of the cow, which moves round and round threshing the corn. This nail is called בן גרן.

NATHANAEL (B. AL FAYYŪMI (?) OF YAMAN).

One of the sections in Prof. Kokovzov's volume contains a fragment of a Hebrew-Arabic grammar. It is written in Arabic, but in Hebrew characters. All we learn concerning the author is that he alludes to himself several times as Nathanael, and only from some orthographic peculiarities may we gather that the work was written in Yaman. The Introduction to a work on philosophy by Nathanael b. Al Fayyūmi was published by Prof. R. Gottheil in the *Festschrift zum achtzigsten Geburtstage Moritz Steinschneiders* (p. 144 sqq.). He suggests with good reason that the author of our fragment was the father of Jacob b. Nathanael al-Fayyūmi, to whom Maimuni addresses his *Letter of Consolation.* A further proof is the fact that the author of this grammatical treatise is philosophically inclined, beginning his work with Aristotle's definition of 'the sentence', and adding that David anticipated this definition in Ps. 139. 4. He also quotes Aristotle's *Poetics.* The work itself is a Hebrew grammar on an Arabic grammar, as is seen from the heading of the first chapter—*Definition of the sentence according to the view of Aristotle and the view of the Arabs.* Then follows a chapter on the *noun* according to the view of Arab grammarians. The following chapters treat on the Hebrew verb, the particles, the imperfect, the corroborative, the permutative, command (positive and negative), the pronouns, and construct state. Even this brief fragment shows that the work must have been of comprehensive character, and that its author was imbued with true scientific spirit.

The detached pronouns expressing the accusative are אותי,[1] &c. אותי is used for masculine as well as feminine (Gen. 12. 12; 2 Sam. 14. 16). The same is the case in the plural in Deut. 6. 23. The masculine of the *second* person is אוֹתְךָ (Gen. 7. 1; 2 Kings 8. 13); feminine אוֹתָךְ (Gen. 12. 12). The *third* person is אוֹתוֹ (Lev. 1. 11; 2 Sam. 12. 9); fem. אוֹתָהּ (Judg. 14. 3; Ezek. 32.16). *Second* person plur. is אֶתְכֶם (Deut. 4.20); fem. אֶתְכֶן (*sic*) (Amos 4. 2) *Third* person plur. אותם (Gen. 1. 22, 28).

On the genitive construction:[2] 'When the Arabs make a noun dependent on another which stands in the genitive, they deprive it of the definite article, while they mark the second noun with the vowel of the genitive. The first noun loses its *nunation*, and the נ in dual and plural. The Hebrews put the two nouns together, e.g. עוף השמים, מזבח הנחשת, חול הים, עץ השדה, בגד תכלת. The (Arab) grammarians do not employ the definite article with the dependent noun, because no noun is doubly determined, so that the first of the two nouns has no article. If in Hebrew the first noun has the article, e.g. ואת הכבש אחד (Num. 28. 4, את ההר שמרון (1 Kings 16. 24), it is unusual, while in common construction the first noun stands without the article, but becomes definite (through the construction), e.g. מַלְכֵי הארץ, &c. Both the Arab as well as Hebrew grammarians put two determined nouns together, as in כל העם הנותר (1 Kings 9. 20; 2 Chron. 8. 7); מי האיש החכם (Jer. 9. 11), והכסף יענה את הכל (Eccl. 10. 19), נגע הצרעת מן הצרוע (Lev. 14. 3). Two indeterminate nouns meet in בית און (Hos. 4. 15; 5. 8), עץ פרי (Gen. 1. 11), &c., and even three, e.g. Job 20. 17; 2 Sam. 20. 19, &c. Hebrew also admits a preposition, e.g. מרעת יושבי בה (Jer. 12. 4; Ps. 107. 34), &c., and puts cognate things together, e.g. כלי עץ (Lev. 11. 32) irrespective of determinate or indeterminate nouns, e.g. איש הדמים (2 Sam. 16. 7) and אנשי דמים (Ps. 55. 24), &c., &c.

[1] Kokovzov, p. 184 (Arab)..

[2] ibid., p. 186.

CHAPTER VIII

Abraham b. Ezra, Judah Hadāsi, Solomon Parḥōn.

It is a noteworthy fact that just as in Rome the old uncritical system lingered longest so there it came to a definite end. For while Menaḥem b. Solomon was busy compiling his work a man had taken up his abode in that city who inaugurated as well as propagated the scientific study of Hebrew grammar no longer in Arabic but in Hebrew. This was Abraham b. Ezra. Born in Toledo near the end of the eleventh century, he united Hebraic with Arabic culture. He excelled as Biblical exegete, as poet, both liturgical and lyrical, but particularly as grammarian. His talent for linguistic exploits permeates all his productions, and is much in evidence in his commentaries on Books of the Bible. His special books on grammar are numerous, although he did not begin writing any of them till he had attained the age of forty. His first treatise, styled *Mōznayim*,[1] was written in Rome. The preface contains a valuable survey of older Jewish doctors of this discipline, and many a name would have fallen into complete oblivion had it not found a place in these pages. The *Mōznayim* may be styled an introduction to the study of Hebrew grammar. It is in the main a dissertation on grammatical definitions composed after the manner of the works of Arab authors, whose writings he states he has studied. Its material, however, yields a complete grammar. A curious feature of this work, as indeed of all Ibn Ezra's writings, is the astrological tint, from which he is unable to detach himself. Thus he explains the horizontal position of the *pathaḥ*, because it recalls the 'encompassing sphere'

[1] See Bacher, *Ibn Ezra als Grammatiker*, Budapest, 1881.

which comprehends all movements.[1] From this scholastic conception of the nature of a vowel sign we can gather that the superlinear system of vowel points remained unknown to him, as it was to all European grammarians.

Discussing the word צין (Ezek. 7. 10), Ibn Ezra alludes to grammarians' who derive this form from a triliteral root (fol. 223 r°.). It is pretty clear that he here alluded to Ḥayyūj. It is, therefore, quite possible that this with other instances suggested to him the translation of this author's two treatises into Hebrew in order to abolish obsolete theories for students outside Spain.[2] He supplemented these works by adding a translation of Ḥayyūj's ספר הנקוד, which up to then had not been attempted. In 1145 Ibn Ezra was in Lucca, where he found leisure to write a small treatise in defence of Sa'adyāh's lexicographical essay against Dūnāsh's criticism. The title of the book is שפת יתר, and he wrote it out of respect for the Gaon rather than from scientific necessity. It is chiefly a protest against Dūnāsh's arrogant manner, and was probably penned under the fresh impression of Ibn Ezra's first perusal of the pamphlet. Nevertheless, Ibn Ezra is frequently compelled to agree with Dūnāsh. In some instances he remained neutral, while in others he rejected the opinion of both in favour of one of his own, as will be seen later on, when it will also be shown that this little book deserves a place among valuable grammatical treatises.

What may have induced Ibn Ezra to compose shortly afterwards another small book on grammar? Of his earlier works probably only a few copies were in circulation, and we hardly do him an injustice by suggesting that he disposed of them to gain a livelihood. From the poetic allusion in the book we may gather that he was already advanced in years when he wrote it. Since no special reason exists for its composition so shortly after its predecessor, it becomes probable that he wrote it for the reason just sug-

[1] The connecting link is formed by the word תנועה 'vowel'.

[2] See above under Moses b. Chiqatilla.

gested. He styled it יסוד הדקדוק.[1] It is an elementary text book, and was probably intended for a beginner. This may account for the circumstance that it remained unknown for centuries, and has only lately been re-discovered,[2] though not published. Nor is there much to be gained by its publication. As a grammarian Ibn Ezra is reproductive rather than productive, and although he fully mastered the linguistic material available in his time from its various sources, he carried it no further. Comparative study in which several of his predecessors indulged he never attempted. He probably shared the fate of many scholars whom dire necessity prevented from following their inclination and forced to provide pot-boilers. At any rate, his is the merit that he was more active than anybody else in promoting the study of Hebrew grammar, and spreading it in European countries outside the Pyrenees.

According to his own testimony he wrote in his later years a new book, in which he claims to have answered all questions that might puzzle a student of Hebrew. This book seems to be an abstract of a more comprehensive work. Its tendency is to teach 'correctness' in the handling of the Hebrew language, and is therefore styled *Ṣāḥōth.* Very characteristic is the beginning, which places the vowel signs on a basis of scholastic cosmology. Being familiar with Arabic grammar he could not fail to lay stress on the fact that the Hebrew vowel system is built on the three primitive vowels *a*, *i*, *u*. A lengthy discussion of the derived vowels forms the first part of the book. This is followed by a classification of the consonants, of which the four gutturals occupy the first place. A rather fine observation is that ח and ע are never found in close proximity. Here he also reveals his extensive acquaintance with Arab grammarians by an allusion to an Arab work entitled 'On the '*ayn*'. Somewhat quaint is his protest that the theories he advanced concerning the shapes and names of the con-

[1] 'Elements of Grammar', Cod. Montefiore, 316 (my *Descriptive Catalogue*, No. 404).

[2] By Pinsker.

sonants were entirely his own, and not learnt from any teacher or book, and he challenges later authors to produce better ones, he having been the first to show the way. In the next chapter he discusses the nouns, the numerals, and the verb in its various inflexions. He does not give a dry scheme of paradigms, but inserts frequent exegetical remarks of striking originality, such as are often to be met with in his commentaries on Biblical books. The *Ṣāḥōth* is concluded by a special paragraph devoted to such expositions, both morphological and syntactic.

The following is a characteristic specimen of the book:

> The little *pataḥ* (*seghōl*) is composed of *little qāmeṣ* (*ṣērē*) and *great pataḥ* (*pataḥ*), and so it is read in the East. Its shape is two dots to indicate the *little qāmeṣ*, and they put a dot underneath in the middle to produce a small sphere as it were, as I have shown thee. For the *great pataḥ* corresponds to the movement of the sphere, while the majority of the little *pataḥs* have a visible quiescent which is *shᵉwā* (*quiescent*), while every vowel ends in either a visible or invisible quiescent.

During his stay in Béziers, Ibn Ezra wrote a small treatise of eight chapters forming a mixture of grammar and philosophy to discuss the nature of the proper noun and the adjective. It is styled ספר השם, and deals with the various appellations of God, at the same time discussing the metaphysical character of the numerals *one* and *ten*. The letter י, he says, not only looks like a semicircle, but also stands for the truth of the Sphere which encompasses the other nine. א and י are kindred to one another even in grammar, because the former as prefix and the latter as suffix represent the first person in verb and noun.[1] The Decalogue begins with אנכי. This remark leads to a theological review of the quiescent letters of which the Tetragrammaton is composed, as well as of the nature of the latter.

Although the *Ṣāḥōth* contains a chapter on the numerals,

[1] e.g. אכתב and ידי.

Ibn Ezra recapitulates it in a special monograph entitled יסוד מספר, *The Element of the Numeral*, both cardinal and ordinal, and the forms derived therefrom. On the paragraph on *eleven* he takes pains, here as well as in the *Ṣāḥōth*, to correct Ibn Janāḥ's explanation of עשתי עשר as על שתי עשר.

For the benefit of a certain Solomon, presumably a benefactor, Ibn Ezra composed his last grammatical essay called שפה ברורה, *Pure Speech*. It bears some resemblance to the *Ṣāḥōth*, as intimated by the title. It is introduced by a somewhat lengthy discourse on a topic which also occupied the minds of earlier authorities, viz. that Hebrew is the oldest language.[1] He strives to refute the theory of the greater antiquity of Aramaic, replacing it by the more correct view that Hebrew, Aramaic, and Arabic form one tongue. Among other arguments he points out that the rule concerning the numerals *three* to *ten* is the same in all three dialects, the first place belonging to Hebrew.

Before entering on his subject proper Ibn Ezra takes the opportunity of passing a rather strict censure on Rashi's exegetical manner, blaming him for his inclination to prefer agadic interpretation to the elucidation of the plain meaning of the text. Rashi, he says, has adopted the latter course in a few instances only. Ibn Ezra proves the justice of his criticism by extracting a number of passages. He then proceeds to lay down a number of exegetical remarks comparing certain passages with the Targum and the explanations of Ibn Janāḥ. At the end of the discourse he mentions the titles of his previous works on grammar, and the places in which they were written. Finally, he states the reason of the composition of this new one, alleging that the persons for whose benefit they were written had no access to others.

Judah Hadāsi, the Qaraite. This concluding remark of Ibn Ezra must not be taken literally. In the middle of the

[1] See *Qirqisani Studies*, p. 24.

twelfth century the Qaraite Judah Hadāsi in Constantinople wrote his large work אשכול הכופר (*Clusters of Grapes*), in which he embodied an elaborate grammar.[1] His anti-rabbanite bias did not prevent him from being a follower of Ḥayyūj and Ibn Janāḥ, whose works he quotes. He also mentions Ibn Ezra, whom he seems to have held in such respect that he adds to his name the eulogy attached to defunct persons. As the latter died in 1167, Hadāsi's statement that his work was written in 1149 either rests on a misprint in the edition, or only gives the year when the work was begun. Of greater interest are his allusions to grammatical works by *Sahl b. Maṣlīaḥ*, *Abul Sari*,[2] a work called מאירת עינים, and a *Sēpher Harūni*.[3] Otherwise this grammar, which is written in the dull rhyming style of the whole work is of no literary interest, except perhaps the paragraphs on the denominative verbs.[4]

SOLOMON PARḤŌN.

As if to allay Ibn Ezra's despondency his most prominent pupil, Solomon Parḥōn of Aragon, stepped into the breach. He supplemented his teacher's writings by the composition of a new grammar, adding a dictionary, and giving both works the comprehensive title *Maḥbereth He 'Ārūkh*. The work was completed in 1160. 'I saw', he says in the preface, 'Menaḥem's dictionary in the hands of, and much praised by, some people, and . . . noticed the lack of fuller explanations on the part of those prominent authors who wrote in Arabic, viz. Ḥayyūj, Sa'adyāh, Ibn Janāḥ, and Samuel Hannāgīd. When I settled in Salerno and found that none of these works was known there I resolved to translate them into Hebrew, not indeed independently, but to utilize the material for *Ārūkh* with comments. When in difficulties I consulted my teachers, R. Ephraim, Judah

1 Begun 1149; printed Eupatoria, 1836.
2 Cp. *Al Hīti*, ed. Margoliouth, pp. 10–14.
3 Evidently Abul Faraj Hārūn.
4 ותהינו, see p. 81.

Hallēvi, Ibn Ezra, and others.' This extract is interesting from more than one point of view. It not only provides the name of an otherwise unknown grammarian of high standing, but it bears testimony to the esteem in which Judah Hallēvi's phonological dissertation was held.[1] Finally, we learn from it something about the personal relation of Parḥōn to Ibn Ezra, whom he apparently met and adopted as teacher at Salerno.

The chief value of Parḥōn's work is that he continued Ibn Ezra's endeavours to make the older authorities accessible to those who knew no Arabic, not by translations (as Ibn Ezra had done with Ḥayyūj's two treatises), but by a work which anticipated Judah b. Tibbon's Hebrew translation of Ibn Janāḥ's double volume by about ten years. Parḥōn's work is introduced by a reproduction of Solomon b. Gabirol's poem on grammar discussed previously.[2] The grammatical part follows pretty closely Ibn Janāḥ's grammar, and the dictionary is so arranged that all nouns consisting of more than three consonants are placed at the end of each section. The resemblance between the two works is so great that Ibn Tibbon erroneously ascribes to him 'the third translation' of these books.[3] To Ibn Tibbon we also owe the acquaintance of the names of two grammarians of whose writings nothing is known at present. The one is Isaac Hallevi, to whom he not only ascribes the Hebrew translation of about half of Ibn Janāḥ's dictionary (letters *āleph* to *lāmedh*), but also the authorship of a work styled *Sēpher Hammāqōr*. Whether this deals with the infinitive or the word *māqōr* has some wider meaning is uncertain. All that Ibn Tibbon says on this point is that Isaac compiled in this work rules on linguistic matter and the inflexion of the verb.[4]

1 See *Al Khazari*, II, 80.
2 See above, p. 49.
3 *Kitab al Uṣūl*, p. 550, also mentioning Isaac Hallevi of Barcelona.
4 *Riqmāh*, ed. Goldberg, p. ii.

CHAPTER IX

The Qimḥi Family.

In the second half of the twelfth century a new movement began which aimed at making the works of Jewish authors written in Arabic more accessible to readers in Europe outside the East and Spain than they had been hitherto. Perhaps it was the example set by Ibn Ezra's translation of Ḥayyūj's writings which induced the Spaniard Joseph b. Isaac Qimḥi, then living in Narbonne, to present his co-religionists with a Hebrew version of Baḥyā b. Baqūda's *Duties of the Hearts,* as well as a metrical reproduction of the *Choice of Pearls*, attributed to Ibn Gebirol.[1] From these he proceeded to turn his attention to grammar, to which he devoted two treatises. In the first, styled *Book of Remembrance*,[2] the influence of Ibn Ezra is visible, because in one of the introductory poems the title of the latter's שפת יתר is interwoven in one of the lines.

Ibn Ezra had done his best to spread the knowledge of Hebrew in various countries of Christian Europe. It might, therefore, be surprising that almost immediately after his disappearance the Qimḥis thought it necessary to supplement his writings with new works. As a matter of fact their efforts were not superfluous, and many whose calling demanded a close acquaintance with the holy tongue were lacking in the knowledge of its very elements. The evil must have been very great, and is faithfully reflected in the twenty-first Maqāma of Judah al Ḥarīzi's Tahkemōni. The poet describes his visit to the synagogue of a great eastern city, which from his description seems to have

[1] See H. Gollancz, שקל הקדש, London, 1918.

[2] Mal. 3. 16.

been Baghdād. He pours scorn on the profound ignorance of the Reader, and even if we make allowances for poetic exaggeration the fact remains that in the birthplace of Hebrew grammar the knowledge of the rules of Hebrew had not found much encouragement.

Joseph Qimḥi's book is a sketch of Hebrew grammar. In the Introduction he explains the term *'ibri* in the same manner as Judah Hallēvi in the book *Alkhazari.*[1] He then speaks of the classification, interchange, and assimilation of consonants, and their functions when placed at the beginning or end of a vowel. He proceeds, however, in so mechanical a manner that he takes, e. g. the preposition ל before an infinitive as a formative letter. In the additional א at the end of certain verbal forms he finds an analogy to the *āleph otiosum* in Arabic. The verbal conjugations are next briefly touched upon. His discussion of the vowels is thoroughly scholastic. He counts *ten* vowels, five long and five short ones. This shows how far his system travelled under the influence of the Māsōrāh from the original Semitic vowel system, which only knows three vowels, viz. *a*, *i*, and *u*. He emphasizes the rule that the *Sh*ᵉ*wā mobile* is in certain instances read with a slight reverberation of the following vowel.[2] This is followed by a classification of the noun, and a survey of the numeral. An elaborate chapter on the inflexion of the noun forms the concluding section. The work ends with six lines of poetry. The work has now only a literary interest. It is as much a help for beginners as Ibn Ezra's grammar books, and offers, therefore, hardly any scope for historical criticism. Of a different stamp is Joseph Qimḥi's next work, which he composed at the age of sixty, and which he styled *Sēpher Haggālūy.*[3] It is addressed to students who are

[1] II, 68, see my English translation, p. 124.

[2] Sephardi tradition reads *a* after ga'yāh; cp. Blüth, 'Joseph Kimḥi und seine Grammatik', *Magazin f. d. Wissensch. d. Judenth*, 1891; Bacher, *R.É.J.*, VI, 208.

[3] Jer. 32. 14, where the term really means an unsigned document; cf Bacher, p. 74 rem. The work was edited by H. J. Mathews, Berlin, 1887.

acquainted with the earlier literature and all the questions connected with the study of the Hebrew language.

The study of the Tōrāh, the author says at the beginning, requires the study of its speech, because he whom God has favoured to study the Talmud successfully, and has learned from the mouth of the great teachers, and is familiar with the intricacies of Holy Writ, even external matters such as poetry like R. Hāi and Isaac Ghayyāth (who were adepts in the Talmud as well as in grammar), should follow their example. He then proceeds by giving a list of his predecessors. It is, however, curious to note that he omits Sa'adyāh, but mentions Moses b. Ezra's work on *Rhetoric*, although this does not, strictly speaking, deal with questions of language. He acknowledges his indebtedness to his father, who was his principal teacher, and introduced him to the works of the earlier authorities and the differences in their opinions.

The purpose of the book is a return to a critical treatment of Menaḥem's dictionary. It is rather astonishing that at this juncture, and so long after the publication of Ibn Janāḥ's great work of the same character, a retrogression of this kind should have taken place, and although Joseph Qimḥi quotes this work. The opportunity of using it, however, was lacking, because the majority of Bible students in Europe were unable to read it in the original. Apart from this, it was Rashi's great fame which secured Menaḥem's work unrivalled authority in western Europe. Joseph Qimḥi subjected it to a fresh examination. His work consists of two parts. In the first he criticizes Menaḥem's expositions, together with Dūnāsh's and Jacob Tām's annotations, and in the second a number of other paragraphs not touched upon by these two critics. A curious feature of the book is that it was handed down to posterity accompanied by the notes of a certain Benjamin,[1]

[1] Not to be confounded with Benjamin b. Judah, author of an introduction to Moses Qimhi's מהלך ; see further on.

whose identity is not disclosed, but who was undoubtedly a scholar of no mean attainments.

Joseph Qimḥi betrays his independence by the fact that, so far from always agreeing with Dūnāsh, he occasionally upholds Menaḥem's view against him. The uncertainty prevailing as to the etymology of many Hebrew forms, even in modern works, naturally produced diversity of opinions in those times of less mature comprehension of the inner working of the Hebrew language. Instead of dwelling on this point at any length it is preferable to illustrate the controversy by a few specimens.

וַתָּהִינוּ[1] (Deut. 1. 41) is derived by Menaḥem from הִן, as in Num. 14. 44. Dūnāsh, rejecting this explanation, gives it the meaning of תאיצו (Isa. 22. 4). Jacob Tām is undecided, but Joseph Qimḥi (p. 36) sides with Menaḥem. He was justified in so doing as there are many parallels of forms derived from particles, such as אָפוּנָה (Ps. 88. 16), which is derived from פֵּן, and for which reason the derivation from הִן is possible. The assertion of Dūnash that particles cannot be used verbally, is vanity and wind.

וְעוֹרְקַי (Job 30. 17) explained by Menaḥem like הָעוֹרְקִים צִיָּה (ibid., 30. 3) as Targum hath it: *they flee*. Dūnāsh (p. 85) divides the two instances, giving the second one the Arabic meaning of *sinews*. Jacob Tām as well as Joseph Qimḥi (pp. 51 and 135) agree with Menaḥem.

The second part of the *Sēpher Haggālūy*,[2] which was probably written after a lengthy interval, and was meant to be published under a different title, discusses a large number of items in Menaḥem's dictionary (as remarked above) on the basis of our author's independent research. For this reason some paragraphs previously treated in the earlier part are again investigated, and augmented by fresh arguments.[3] In various paragraphs the author is, in his turn, criticized by Benjamin, but it is to be noted that this name only occurs four times, and only in the early

[1] See also Sa'adyāh's explanation in my article, *J.Q.R.*, 1916, p. 58.

[2] See ed., p. 101, where the author quotes the work by its own title.

[3] e.g. מסכן, pp. 46 and 119.

part of the work. The arrangement is alphabetical. The following are a few specimens:

(p. 121). נִין (Isa. 14. 22), which the author groups together with נִינם (Ps. 74. 8) and explains: *let us oppress them*, as in Lev. 25. 17, but this is a Qal-form like וַנִּירָם (Num. 21. 30), which means: *we shot at them*, from the root ירה (Exod. 15. 4), whilst לא תונו is from הונה.

(p. 129). 1. עֵט סוֹפֵר (Ps. 45. 2); 2. עוטה אור (Ps. 104. 2) the root being עטה as in מעטה (Ezek. 21. 20), as I remarked before (p. 47). I investigated the whole subject, and found that it (מעוטה) is the same form as מעונה from ענה, מכוסה from כסה, מעוטה from עטה. He (Menaḥem) classes it with וַיַּעַט (1 Sam. 14. 32), the root of which is עָטָה, but not with וַיָּעַט (ibid., 25. 14), which belongs to עִיט. The meaning is: he *made them hurry* (*with threat*), from the root עיט. The י of ויעט has *pataḥ*, as in וַיַּעַן, וַיַּעַשׂ, while the י in וַיָּעַט has *qāmeṣ* and in וַיָּקָם of the class ע"ו.

Moses Qimḥi. Joseph Qimḥi's two sons and pupils, Moses and David, especially the latter, gained renown as the authors of school-books on grammar and lexicography. Moses composed only one book, known as מהלך,[1] but it became so famous that it was edited with a commentary by the celebrated Elijah Levita, Pesaro, 1508, and reprinted about ten times during the sixteenth century alone. Subsequent editions, some of them by renowned grammarians such as Sebastian Münster and others, followed, the last edition being Hamburg, 1785. In variation of the method of his father it begins with a classification of the noun into substantive, adjective, relative noun, and numeral. Like his father he counts *ten* vowels, and three parts of speech, viz. noun, verb, and particle. Of reading rules and phonology only as much is given as is necessary for young pupils, while the paradigm of the verb with the pronominal suffixes is treated very fully. It is a useful rather than ambitious work.

[1] The full title is מַהלך שְׁבילי הַדעת, the initial letter of each word yielding the name of the author.

David Qimḥi (born 1160) was the youngest member of the family, but eclipsed both his father and elder brother in his scientific achievements, to which belong his commentaries on Biblical books. Before entering into the discussion of his activity as a grammarian an interesting literary puzzle must be disposed of. There exists an essay on grammar beginning פתח דְּבָרַי, handed down anonymously. The grammarian Abraham de Balmes [1] ascribes the work to *our* David Qimḥi. The late Professor Bacher, in a special study of the question,[2] denies this emphatically. We are in possession of a grammatical treatise by *Meir b. Solomon b. David*,[3] who in the preface refers to his grandfather, 'the author of פתח דברי'.

Now it might appear rash to identify this grandfather with David Qimḥi. Unfortunately we do not know when this Meir b. Solomon lived, but he probably wrote in the earlier part of the fourteenth century. From the chronological point of view his near descent from David Qimḥi could, then, hardly be contested. Abraham de Balmes' assertion, very likely based on good information, has much in its favour. Apart from this, it is strange that the author of the פתח דברי should have left his book without title or name, just as a teacher would keep his notes for academic lectures. Why did he not simply have his father's or his brother's books copied for the benefit of his pupils? He says in his preface, among other interesting observations: 'As the youngest in the house of my father and family I composed for my pupils . . . a plain book calculated for

[1] מקנה אברהם, see below. [2] *RÉJ.*, 1884, pp. 140 sqq.

[3] Cod. Montefiore, 157, 3 (Cat., No. 410): אני מאיר בר שלמה בר דוד הקטן באלפי והצעיר בבית אבי לבאר ענינים הוצרכתי לבארם לטרדת מבוכות הזמן אשר אתי בל תשכיחם ממני לחוסר דעתי ולקוצר יד שכלי וברשום בכתב אמת לנוכח פני שמתים להשגת משכילי בעוד ידעתים והם אשר עזב אבי זקני ולא זכרם בחבורו פתח דברי להשענו על רוב חכמתו ואשר בזמנו על נקלה יבינום הבחורים ואני אשר יאות לי חכמות שבתי עליהם ובינותי בספרים ובארתים ושמותם שבעה שערים:

their needs.' It was evidently not meant to be a learned treatise, but consisted of notes to be dictated. For this reason the chapters on the inflexion of the verb are placed in the beginning, opening with the unassuming remark: *The beginning of my words.* That it then launches forth in the praise of God was but following a time-honoured custom. I therefore suggest that the book represents David Qimḥi's earliest attempt to compile a manual of Hebrew grammar. Any contemporary author would have taken care to give fuller information concerning his identity.

David laid down the results of his linguistic studies in a work consisting of two parts, a grammar and a dictionary, both under the common title *Mikhlōl.* As regards the grammar, it is not only larger than the *Petaḥ Debhāray,* but its composition and whole system show that it was not meant for beginners. The author frequently quotes his father and brother (both of whom were no longer alive), but all the old authorities, adding Isaac Ghayyāth, Isaac Chiqatilla,[1] and Aliy (Ēli ?) b. Hannazīr, and Jacob b. El'azar, of both of whom, however, nothing has as yet come down to us. Several times he refers to a Jerusalem codex of the Bible he had seen, compares Aramaic passages, Mishnah, Targum, Māsōrāh, and the *Sēpher Yeṣīrāh.* In other places he adds exegetical, halākhic, and agādic notes. The etymology of שבת caused him the same perplexity as it does to modern grammarians.[2] Of special interest is his observation on two identical consonants standing in close proximity. He polemizes against Ibn Janāḥ's assertion that the Law demands a clear pronunciation of both consonants only in the reading of the *Shema',* while in other portions the assimilation of such and even cognate consonants is permissible.

The Rabbi's prohibition, he says,[3] refers to the whole of the Bible, which it is our duty to read. This being so, all letters must be pronounced distinctly. Their prohibition concerning

[1] See Steinschneider, *Arab. Lit.,* p. 121.
[2] See my article in *Journ. Roy. As. Soc.* 1896, p. 353 sqq.
[3] fol. 80 v°.

the *Sh'ma'* was for two reasons: one is that these paragraphs contain the unification of the name of God, and the acceptance of the 'yoke of commandments'. The other reason is that all Israel read these chapters twice every day, the learned and the unlearned. People must therefore be careful in the reading because of the unlearned, who are unskilled in reading. Another reason for the demand of distinct pronunciation of letters is lest the meaning of one be not like that of the other, as they said: The ז of תִּזְכְּרוּ must not be spoken like ס.[1]

Just as in the *Petaḥ Debharay*, the bulk of the book is devoted to the verb. In the chapter on verbs with a weak radical is inserted a discussion on the phonetic effect of these letters with double pronunciation. Quoting a passage from the *Sēpher Yēṣīrāh* that ר belongs to the same group, he states (fol. 90 v°.) that he has seen in a volume by Aliy b. Judah Hannāzīr that hard or soft pronunciation of ר is strictly adhered to by the 'Children of Ma'azyāh in Tiberias' only.[2] A special chapter is given to doubtful roots with double consonants, which are recommended for further study. The chapters on the noun and particle are placed in the latter part of the book. Owing to its thoroughness and critical manner the book became very popular, and was considered authoritative for centuries, the last edition having been published as late as Lyck, 1864.

The second part of the *Mikhlōl* is the dictionary styled *Book of Roots*, a title probably modelled on, if not borrowed from, Ibn Janāḥ's work mentioned before. It is not superfluous to examine the *raison d'être* of the work, since Judah b. Tibbon's Hebrew version of Ibn Janāḥ's work saw the light at Lunel at a time when David Qimḥi was a little boy (1170). The Spaniard Solomon Parḥōn's dictionary, mentioned before, does not seem to have come under his notice; at any rate he never mentions it. This is another instance showing the circumscribed area in which works circulated prior to the printing press. We can only assume that David Qimḥi composed this rival work to Ibn

[1] Berakhōth, fol. 15 v°.

[2] Neh. 10. 9; 1 Chron. 24. 18.

Janāḥ's because he felt that he too had something to say. As a matter of fact he frequently contradicts and even corrects Ibn Janāḥ, and instead of publishing a criticism, as Dūnāsh and his own father had done in the case of Menaḥem, he preferred to examine the whole Hebrew vocabulary afresh. A comparison of both works is an interesting and fruitful task. Needless to say he quotes all the old authorities. In two places he quotes Maimonides' *Mōrēh.*[1] Among his father's writings he mentions a חבור הלקט,[2] of which, however, nothing is at present known. His constant references to Arabic roots not only manifest his critical spirit, but lead to interesting results.[3] He also kept a watchful eye on the language of the Prayer Book. He blames liturgical poets for shortening בַּעֲבוּר into עֲבוּר, and passes strict censure on the phrase תֵּעָנוּ וְתֵעָתְרוּ at the conclusion of prayers on the Day of Atonement. His dictionary marks a distinct progress in Hebrew lexicography. It is not only wellnigh exhaustive as to material and clearly written, but it abounds in exegetical remarks. Owing to its rapidly increasing popularity it was frequently copied and extracted, and was the first of all writings of a Qimḥi committed to the press (Naples, 1490). Edition followed edition, the last one being published with Elijah Heller's annotations, Berlin, 1847.[4]

As a supplement to his linguistic writings David left a small essay, grammatical and masoretic, which he styled *'Ēṭ Sōphēr.*[5] Its purpose is to provide writers of Scripture with the rules necessary for their work. It begins with a note on the *qᵉrē* and *kᵉthībh*, then gives a complete though brief abstract of the grammar, and concludes with a survey of the accents.

[1] *Le Guide*, III, p. 152 (ch. XXIX). [2] p. 279.

[3] e.g. גלשו, Cant. 4. 1. This he refers with Ibn Janāḥ to Arabic גלס (غلس) which is an important proof that the work of the latter was written in Hebrew characters.

[4] edd. Lebrecht and Biesenthal, Berlin, 1847. As to a compendium see Neubauer, Cat., No. 1482.

[5] ed. Goldberg, Lyck, 1864.

CHAPTER X

Tanḥūm of Jerusalem, Abraham b. Isaac of Béziers, Moses b. Isaac Hannesīāh.

ALTHOUGH Maimonides evinced no active interest in linguistic pursuits, he stimulated it indirectly if we take the opening chapters of his *Mōreh* as contributions to the exposition of synonyms. It did not take long for his great legal code, the *Mishnēh Tōrāh,* to reach the East. On account of its aim to supersede the Talmud it had all the greater scope of appealing to the people, as its smaller bulk helped multiplication as well as study. Being, however, written in Hebrew it presented difficulties for an Arabic-speaking population. At present we do not know whether the poet Judāh Al Ḥarizī wrote his *Introduction into the Hebrew Language* [1] with a view to promote the study of Maimonides' work just mentioned, or for general purposes. Unfortunately no relic of this essay is known at present. We are in a better position with regard to another and much more important work by the famous Bible exegete *Tanḥūm of Jerusalem,*[2] who set himself the task to assist the student of the *Mishnēh Tōrāh* by providing a dictionary for it written in Arabic, incidentally including the language of the Mishnāh. The title of the work is the *Adequate Guide.*[3] The usefulness of this work is shown by the circumstance that in spite of its bulk it was frequently copied.

The author was abreast of the latest achievements of his age. His dictionary is not therefore a mere adaptation

[1] See Neubauer, *JA.*, 1862, p. 250.

[2] Steinschneider, *Arab. Lit.*, p. 234.

[3] Almurshid al Kāi.

of Nathan b. Jeḥiel's *'Arūkh,* but based on independent research. Although chiefly designed for the study of the *Mishnēh Tōrāh* the work also includes the vocabulary of the Mishnāh. It has received due attention at the hands of modern scholars.[1] It is therefore only necessary to reproduce here a small specimen which has not been published before:[2]

גמילות חסדים-גמל (so). Bestowing benefits and showing generosity both with money and physical action. The word is used in four different ways. *First:* ordinary *requital,* both in a good and a bad sense, as in Ps. 18. 21 and 28. 4.[3] *Second*: to be *abundantly generous,* used only in a good sense as in Ps. 119. 17; 13. 6. To this category belongs *bestowing benefits* in a physical sense, visiting the sick, attending funerals, seeing one's friends, making them comfortable, &c. *Third*: *weaning* a child (1 Sam. 1. 23; Gen 21. 8). As to Prov. 11. 17, it is explained by some as belonging to No. 2, but No. 3 is more suitable. *Fourth*: tying up, as in Num. 17. 23; Isa. 18. 5. In the Mishnāh the word is used in a different meaning, viz. הגמלונין. אפונין (Kil'āim 3. 2)

[1] See Bacher, *Tanchum Jer.*

[2] Cod. Brit. Mus. Or. 1303, fol. 25 vo. גמל גמילות חסדים אלהילה
באלאפצאל ואצאל אלגמיל ואלמכאום באלמאל ואלגסם ולפטה גמל
פי אלנצוץ תתצמן ארבעה מעאני אלמשהור מנהא אלמכאפה עמא תקדם
כיר או שר ינמלני ייי כצדקי ישוב גמולם להם ותכון אילה ואהסאן בזאיד
מן גיר שי תקדם מנה והדי לא יכון אלי כיר גמול על עבדך אחיה
אשירה לייו כי גמל עלי ויכון הדי אלמעני גמילות חסדים ויכון באלגסם
כזיארה אלמרצא ותשיע אלאמואת וזיארה אלאצחאב פי הנאהם ונחו דלך
ואלמעני אלג אלפטאם עד גמלה אותו ביום הגמל את יצחק ואמא גומל
נפשו איש חסד פבעץ שרחה מן אלמעני אלב וכונה מן הדי אלג אחסן
ואלראבע עקד אלתמאר ויגמל שקדים ובוסר גומל יהיה נצה ומעני אכר
אפונין הגמלונין קד דכר פי חרף אלאלף אנה אלחמץ אלכביר ואן אלשי
אלכביר יסמא גמלא ומנה קולה נשבע אני שראיתי גמל פורח יריד טיר
כביר תגאהיי ופי אלסריאני אסם כלשי כביר כאן מא כאן גמלא

[3] The MS. has ישוב.

has already been mentioned under letter א and is the large-sized pulse. Every big thing is called גמלא. 'I swear I have seen a flying camel', which means a large bird. In Aramaic the name of any large thing is גמלא.

Although belonging to a later period (sixteenth century) it is not out of place to mention here a small glossary on the Mishnāh and Maimonides' last-mentioned work by an unknown Yemenite author. It is an unpretentious compilation embracing only the first two letters of the alphabet. It is largely dependent on Tanḥūm, but it gives some items not found in the larger work. No Biblical passages are quoted. As it has been published there is no need to give any specimens. The book was evidently meant for beginners.[1]

Abraham b. Isaac of Béziers, commonly called Bedarshi, who lived in the latter half of the thirteenth century, struck a new line in a work on the synonyms,[2] styled *Ḥōthām Tokhnīth*[3] ('The Seal of the well-built Edifice'). It consists of twenty-two sections according to the letters of the alphabet, each section being divided into paragraphs. These are headed by groups of words which have some general meaning in common. Each word is then explained lexicographically, and illustrated by a number of quotations from the Bible. It is hardly necessary to say that the author was conversant with the works of the old authorities, Menaḥem and Dūnāsh, and especially Ibn Janāḥ and Solomon Parḥōn. The latter are mentioned by name in the introductory poem. The following specimen will give a fair notion of the character of the work:

אד, עב, ענן. The first word is sufficiently explained by Ibn Janāḥ (see Gen. 2. 6), and speaks of the *mist* that rises from the ground like smoke. When this is very high it becomes

[1] ed. N. M. Nathan, *Ein anonymes Wörterbuch und Jad haḥasaka*, Berlin, 1905.

[2] Not to be confounded with Judah b. Bal'am's work on homonyms.

[3] Bacher, p. 88, reads *ḥōthēm*, 'Besiegler', but see the Māsōrā; the book was edited by G. J. Polak, Amsterdam, 1865.

damp and watery, as in Job 36. 27. In a similar way the word is also used for *grief* and *distress*, as in Job 31. 3; Prov. 1. 26; Ps. 18. 19; Obad. 13; Deut. 32. 35, all being derived from the same root,[1] because grief and distress are like a cloudy and dark mist that covers people. עב is a *thick cloud*, as Rashi explains in Exod. 19. 9, viz. in *the thickness of a cloud* or *fog*, like Deut. 4. 11. ערפל is the same, only עב is more intense than ענן, because the former draws water from the sea, while the latter is lighter, and becomes bright by pouring its water out.

Another linguist of the period who wrote under the influence of Ibn Janāḥ and Parḥōn was *Moses b. Isaac b. Hannesīāh* of London. His aim was to fill gaps left by these two grammarians. The work is called ספר השהם,[2] and consists of two parts. The first is grammatical, and contains a number of apt remarks on questions of phonology, the use of prepositions, exchange of consonants, and morphology, intermixed with remarks on syntax. The second part is a concise dictionary. To every root the author adds the conjugations with which it is used. Several roots are also explained from their use in the Mishnāh. Occasionally French words are quoted. This part of the work is incomplete, and ends in the letter ע.

[1] But see the dictionaries.

[2] ed. G. W. Collins, London. 1882.

CHAPTER XI

The Naqdānim, Isaac Hallēvi b. El'āzar, The Anonymous of Yaman, Elijah of Carcassonne.

ZUNZ, in *Zur Geschichte und Literatur*, has a chapter on the Naqdanim (*punctatores*). He includes in their number several of the older authorities on grammar, beginning with Menaḥem. In a narrower sense they were the bearers of masoretic studies during the thirteenth and partly fourteenth centuries, not merely for the theoretical study of grammar, but rather for practical application in the reading of Holy Writ. Owing to the uncertainty of dates a chronological order of their lives and works cannot be established. Apart from this many of them are only known by their names, their writings not having come down to us. The following list contains only those about whom some direct or indirect information is available:

Samuel Naqdān or *Dayyān*. According to Steinschneider, who published specimens of his writings, these seemed to have formed part of a masoretic commentary on the Pentateuch.[1]

Moses Naqdān of London,[2] the reputed author of a work styled ספר הנקדן or ספר הקונים.

Zalmān Naqdān, also known under the name *Jequthiel b. Isaac Hakhohen* of Prague. He is the author of a treatise under the title עין הקורא.[3]

Joseph b. Kalonymos[4] is the author of a poem on the accents of Psalms, Proverbs, and Job. It consists of forty-one lines in alphabetical order. The last verses give the author's name as an acrostic.

[1] Kobak's *Jeshurun*, V., p. 146 (Hebr.).

[2] Ascribed by Benjacob to Shimshōn; op. Cod. Montefiore, 102; ed. Frensdorf, Hanover, 1865, and מקראות גדולות, ed., 1526, Heidenheim.

[3] Cod. Brit. Mus. Or. 853; see Appendix III.

[4] ed. Berliner, טעמי אמ"ת בחרוזים.

Shimshōn lived at the end of the thirteenth century. The title of his work is השמשוני.[1] The work is a grammar with paradigms. The author quotes Saʿadyāh.

Isaac Hallēvi b. Elʿāzar wrote a kind of supplement to Ibn Janāḥ's grammar, under the title ס' הרקמה, borrowing the Hebrew title of that work for it.[2]

Mordecai b. Hillēl is the author of a poem on the vowels, which exists in print.[3]

The Anonymous of Yaman. The traveller Jacob Sappir brought a manuscript copy of the Pentateuch written in 1390 to Europe.[4] Its earlier part contains a compendium of Hebrew grammar. The author's acquaintance with the terminology of Arab grammarians is conspicuous throughout the work. Beginning with the letters, he discusses their shapes, adding homiletic comments. It should be noted that he speaks only of the Tiberian shapes of vowels,[5] without mentioning the superlinear system. This is a strange phenomenon in view of the numerous biblical and liturgical manuscripts which have come from Yaman. From this we can only gather that the superlinear system was not popular in that country at the time of our author. It should also be observed that Yamanite manuscripts with superlinear vowels do not betray great age, and the suggestion is not very remote that their vocalization is a mere transcription of Tiberian vowels. If this be the case these manuscripts, upon which far-going conclusions for masoretic studies are based, lose a great deal of their historical value. This chiefly concerns the biblical books and sections of the Targum published on their authority. Our author further deals with the three parts of speech, the formation of sentences, the origin and pronunciation of the letters, vowels and accents, changes of consonants, and nominal forms. Of special interest are the paragraphs on elliptic

[1] Cod. Brit. Mus. Or. 1016.

[2] Also שפת יתר, cp. Nutt's Preface to Ḥayyūj, Cat. Neubauer, 1458, *JA.*, XX, p. 250.

[3] ed. Kohn, *Monatschr.*, XXVI, p. 167.

[4] ed. Derenbourg, *JA.*, 1870, pp. 309 sqq.

[5] pp. 362 sqq.

and redundant phrases.[1] He then gives a list of the eight words in the Bible which are not written but read, while those which are written but not read are placed at the end of the masoretic section. This is followed by a survey of the books of the Bible and the prophets and their works. The book ends with a chapter on the number of letters with quatrains attached to each. These the author attributes to the Gaon Sa'adyāh, but Zunz has suggested with good reason that this was Sa'adyāh b. Joseph Bᵉkhōr Shōr, who lived near the end of the twelfth century.

Elijah b. Isaac of Carcassonne, who lived in the earlier part of the fourteenth century, is the compiler of a large ritual work which bears the title *Asūphōth.*[2] The later part deals with the regulations concerning the rules of writing and reading the Pentateuch. The final chapter is headed אתחיל שערי נקוד and is of grammatical character. It ends with tables of the forms of the imperfect, imperative, and past tenses with and without suffixa.

[1] See *Qirqisāni Studies*, p. 20. Q. often quotes the same instances, e.g. Lev. 14. 3.

[2] Cod. Montefiore, 115 (Cat. No. 134); cp. Gross, *Magazin für die Wissensch. d. Judenth.* X, pp. 64–87, and Gaster, *Report of Montef. College*, 1893, pp. 31 sqq.

CHAPTER XII

Joseph b. Abbā Māri Caspi, Joseph b. David Hayyevāni, Solomon b. Abbā Māri Jarḥāi, Prophiat Dūrān, Judah b. Jeḥīēl, Sa'adyāh b. Danān, Moses b. Shēm Tāb b. Ḥabīb, Māqre Dardeqē, David b. Yaḥyā, Elisha b. Abraham, Samuel b. Jacob, Elijah Levita, Abraham de Balmes.

Joseph b. Abbā Māri Caspi was a very prolific writer on Biblical exegesis, theology, philosophy, and linguistics, who left no less than three treatises on grammar. One of them, styled פריישה (or פרויש), consists of notes on Ibn Janāḥ's grammar, but is apparently lost.[1] The other, called רתוקות כסף (*chains of silver*), consisting of seventy-three chapters on grammar with a dictionary,[2] while the third, bearing the title שרשות כסף (*garlands of silver*), gives a survey of Hebrew roots.[3] As the late Dr. Neubauer has given a full account of the two last-named works, there is no need to offer any further analysis of them, especially as their purpose to improve upon Ibn Janāḥ's and David Qimḥi's writing has not been fulfilled. Copies of Caspi's work are therefore comparatively rare, and as yet unpublished.

To the same period belongs *Joseph b. David Hayyevāni* (the Greek), author of a treatise styled מנורת המאור (*Lamp of Light*). This work is likewise a grammar accompanied by a lexicon. The title of the work appears in an introductory poem. He quotes Ibn Ḥayyūj, Ibn Janāḥ, Moses b. Ezra, and Isaac b. Ela'zar, the author of ס' הרקמה. The work remained incomplete. Like older grammarians, he complains of the neglect of grammatical studies on the part of his contemporaries.[4]

Solomon b. Abbā Māri Jarhāi of Lunel, who lived at

[1] See Neubauer, *Ecr. Juifs français*, p. 482. [2] Ibid., pp. 499 sqq.

[3] Also styled ס' השרשים.

[4] See Duke's, *Ltbl.*, X, pp. 505, 705, 746.

about the middle of the fourteenth century, is the author of a small compendium of grammar styled לשון למודים. In the preface[1] he describes his unhappy life, made still more unhappy by the loss of his eyesight He deplores the general neglect of the study of Hebrew, and consequent ignorance. We gather from this that the writings of Ibn Ezra, and especially the Qimḥis, had not spread outside a narrow circle of students. This state of things induced him to write the treatise. It consists of two parts, the earlier being devoted to phonology, and the latter embracing the verbs, nouns, and particles. The work is nothing but a handbook for beginners.

Propheh (*Prophiat*) *Durān Hallevi* is the author of the famous epistle styled 'Be not like thy Forefathers', addressed to a renegade.[2] The author's full name was Isaac b. Moses, a native of Spain towards the end of the fourteenth century. From the initials of the words אמר פרופייט דוראן; he adopted the name *Ephodi*. In 1503 he completed a work on grammar consisting of thirty-three chapters.[3] After a preface of philosophic character he sets forth fifteen rules to be observed by the student. Among these, three insist on the use of a copy of neat appearance and written in large square characters. The work itself begins with a dissertation on speech, and the superiority of Hebrew over other languages. The author then discusses the consonants and vowels, their changes and various functions, followed by all other divisions of grammar in the time-honoured style. The whole is tinged with a philosophic hue. The following is an extract from the beginning of Chapter VII:

On the decline which befell the Hebrew language after she had been the most perfect speech. Before I speak on the roots of the Hebrew language from which the branches of the speech spread, and the manner of study to be made, I will first say that Hebrew

[1] Cod. Montefiore, 157 (Cat. 410. 3), and Appendix IV.
[2] See Geiger, מקוא חפנים, p. 42.
[3] edd. J. Friedlander and J. Kohn, Vienna, 1865, p. 39.

shared the fate of its users. It declined with their lowly state, and was reduced as they were reduced and forgotten in their exile and unrest.[1] Instead of being, as formerly, the most perfect and copious language, as it should be, it has become the most exiguous, being inadequate in respect of nouns and verbs probably to a very large extent. The great Teacher[2] writes concerning the Unspeakable Name, possible in accordance with the reduced state of the language at our disposal, that we do not know our language, by which he means its imperfect state. The author of the Book, Alkhazari, expresses himself in similar terms.... The doctors of the Talmud left this language, and wrote their words mostly in Aramaic, which is but a corrupt form of the holy tongue. Probably they did so not from choice, but from necessity, because at the time of the composition of the Talmud Hebrew had been forgotten, since this took place more than four hundred years after the destruction [of the Temple], having been concluded in the year 811 of the Era of Documents, i.e. 4259 A. M.

The physician *Judah b. Jeḥīēl* of Mantua, called Messer Leon, wrote in 1454 a work on grammar, in two parts with eleven chapters, under the title לבנת הספיר.[3] A concluding section deals with the accents. He is largely dependent on Ibn Ezra, from whose *Moznayim* he borrowed the definition of the (long) Qāmeṣ as combined of the *Ḥōlem* and *Pataḥ*, which is revealed by its shape. Its name is derived from the form of the mouth in its pronunciation. The people of Tiberias, he concludes, the scholars of Egypt and [North] Africa know how to read the great Qāmeṣ.

Saʿadyāh b. Danān of Granada, returned to the older custom of writing in Arabic. He wrote a grammar, including a treatise on prosody.[4] To this work he added a dictionary. It is significant that the author himself translated the former work into Hebrew, finishing it in 1473. To give two examples of his exegesis, I can only

[1] Evidently borrowed from Judah Hallevi's *Al Khazari*, II. 68; my translation, p. 124.

[2] Maimonides, cp. *Le Guide*, I. 61, 67.

[3] See אוצר נחמד, II, fol. 104; Dukes, *Ltbl.*, VIII, p. 441.

[4] See Neubauer, Cat., No. 1492.

mention that he rejects the derivation of ויאבק (Gen. 32. 25) from אבק, which does not mean 'to throw down', but is connected with חבק. Further, תהכרו (Job 19. 3) means 'to be amazed', or, according to others, 'to be insolent' because this is the meaning of the root in Arabic, and also applies to הכרת פניהם (Isa. 3. 9).

Moses b. Shem Ṭāb Ibn Ḥabīb of Lissabon, who had fled to Italy, is the author of an elementary grammar in form of a catechism, giving it the pompous title מרפא לשון (*Healing of Speech*). In a second treatise, styled דרכי נעם (*Pleasant Ways*), he deals with the rules of prosody. According to the introductory poem the latter work was composed in the year 1486.[1]

A contemporary of the last named was *Solomon b. Abraham* of Urbino. He left a treatise styled אהל מועד on *Homonyms*, arranged as follows: at the head of each section are placed all nouns derived from the same root, followed by explanatory notes and illustrative quotations.[2]

The *Maqrē Dardeqē* (The *Children's Reader*) is a Hebrew-Arabic and Italian glossary, attributed to a certain Jeḥiel,[3] who lived in the fifteenth century either in Italy or in the Provence. This work is evidently the outcome of the interest Jews began to take in the literature of the countries in which they lived, and their wish that their children should become acquainted with the vernacular. Another aim probably was to afford a help to non-Jewish students of Hebrew, and so find in exchange teachers for secular studies.

David b. Yaḥjā, a native of Lissabon (born 1440, died 1506 in Constantinople), wrote a book on grammar for the benefit of a relative of the same name, styling it לשון למודים.[4] In the Introduction he shows himself a disciple

[1] ed. Bomberg, 1564.

[2] Venice, 1548, and again Willheimer, Vienna, 1881.

[3] See Moise Schwab in *RÉJ.*, XVI, p. 252; XVII, 111, 285; Perles, *Beiträge zur Geschichte*, &c., pp. 118 sqq., Munich, 1881; Zedner, Cat., p. 317.

[4] Constantinople, 1506.

and at the same time a critic of David Qimḥi, but a sharper critic of Prophiat Durān, whom he blames partly for undue brevity, partly for prolixity. The chief interest of the book is to be found in the author's remarks on his linguistic pursuits and his studies in other branches of learning. In matters grammatical he has produced nothing new. An appendix to the volume containing this work is a short treatise with the title שקל הקדש, but apparently by a different author, whose identity is not disclosed. The treatise is likewise of an elementary character.

About the same period *Elisha b. Abraham b. Mattithyāhu* wrote a small book mainly in defence of David Qimḥi against his aggressors, especially Ephodi. The title of the work is significantly *Shield of David*.[1] Its literary value is small, but it is a testimony of the hold Qimḥi had on students of the Bible and grammar in particular.

Probably to the same epoch belongs a work by a certain *Samuel b. Jacob*, probably of Italy, bearing the title ראשית הלקח (*Beginning of Learning*). On account of its rarity hardly any notice has hitherto been taken of this work. In the MS. codex Montefiore No. 69[2] it is written on the same page next to Moses Qimḥi's מהלך, on which work it seems to be largely dependent. Another interesting feature is its elaborate system of grammatical definitions, and a terminology which recalls the Latin grammar-book. The author begins with a list of the parts of speech, of which he counts eight, viz. noun, verb, participle, pronoun, preposition, particle, vocative, conjunction. Each of these classes is illustrated by an example. The author's definitions have a philosophic colouring. 'The noun,' he says, 'is the part of speech which points to substance and attribute, either general or individual. Some nouns are either relating to substance or to attribute. The former class indicates a substance without attribute, as *Reuben*, *man*, *earth*, while the latter class indicates a substance qualified by a general attribute as *wise*, *white*, *foolish*, &c.' In this

[1] Constantinople, 1517.

[2] Cat., No. 217 k[2].

manner the author discusses all the following items of his list. Another noteworthy feature in the treatise is the optative,[1] which is evidently borrowed from a classical text-book. On account of its peculiar character the work deserves further attention.

The beginning of the sixteenth century marks a new epoch by the entry of Christian grammarians into the field of the study of Hebrew. In 1506 *John Reuchlin*, himself the pupil of Jewish teachers, published a grammar[2] for the benefit of his co-religionists. It is the first Hebrew grammar produced in Germany.[3] Jewish scholarship in that country concentrated almost exclusively on Rabbinics. This was possibly the reason why *Elijah b. Assher Levita* (born 1469, in a small place near Nuremberg) emigrated to Italy, where grammatical studies flourished at this period. Under the direct influence of Moses Qimḥi his first effort in grammar was devoted to a commentary on the latter's מהלך (published Pesaro, 1508). He then proceeded independently to produce a grammar, which was published under the title ספר הבחור (Rome, 1518). It consists of four sections, the first two dealing with the verb, and the others to the noun. A supplement styled ספר ההרכבה (published in the same year and place) is a kind of explanatory glossary of irregular or obscure verbal and nominal formations arranged in alphabetical order. Two years later appeared his פרקי אליהו, a further supplement to the בחור. It consists of two parts. The *first* is a sketch of grammar in thirteen cantos, with a commentary attached to each, while the *second* part, consisting of two sections with thirteen paragraphs each, gives a classification of nominal forms in their various aspects. He next turned his attention to lexicography, and compiled a glossary of post-biblical words under the title תשבי (Isny 1514),[4] consisting of 712 paragraphs according to the numerical value of the titular word. A parallel

1 תאויי. 2 Pforzheim.

3 Mordecai b. Hillel's (1298) poems are not a grammar.

4 Also published with preface by Paul Fagius: see p. 100, l. 2.

work, being an Aramaic dictionary, was published under the title מתורגמן, with a preface by Paul Fagius, in the same place and year. To these works he added a treatise on the accents, styled טוב טעם (Venice 1538), and his most important work מסורת המסורה (in the same place and year), which proved epoch-making for the study of the Māsorāh. Finally, we should notice his annotations to David Qımḥi's dictionary.[1]

Although Levita did not create any new theories in matters grammatical, he was more successful in his dictionaries, which contain valuable contributions to Hebrew and Aramaic lexicography. In his explanations he often called to his aid German, Italian, and Latin words. Of perhaps greater moment is the stimulus he gave to Christian scholars, who took up the results of his studies with eagerness. The edition of his *Tishbi* was the work of Paulus Fagius. In 1541 the famous Sebastian Münster published a Hebrew grammar[2] confessedly based on Levita's labours. He also edited several of the latter's works with Latin translations. John Mercer edited Judah b. Bal'am's טעמי המקרא Paris, 1565.[3]

Strange to say, while Levita's works were published in Pesaro and Rome, another Jewish grammarian, *Abraham b. Meir de Balmes*, produced a work which appeared with a Latin translation by Bomberg (Venice, 1523). This author also betrays the direct influence of Moses Qimḥi, but shows more originality than Levita. He has a large chapter on phonology, the nature and change of consonants and vowels, classification and formation of nouns, and the use of numerals. The verb is treated in great detail, and is followed by a chapter on syntax. In the chapter on prefixed letters and conjunctions he inserts a note on the double nature of the copulative *wāw*, revealing a fine gift of observation. The work appeals more than many of its

[1] Venice, 1546–8.

[2] Under the title מלאכת הדקדוק השלם, Basle, 1541.

[3] Edited by Jellinek, Leipzig, 1853.

predecessors to the critical faculty of students, and perhaps for this very reason did not enjoy the popularity of the handbooks of Ibn Ezra, David Qimḥi, and Levita, which proved of greater practical value for the beginner.

Judah b. Jeḥiēl (also known as *Messer Leon*), Rabbi and physician at Mantua, in the middle of the fifteenth century, wrote a work on grammar styled לבנת הספיר. It consists of eleven chapters, with an additional chapter on the accents. The work is devoid of original research, being in the main based on the writings of Ibn Ezra. A manuscript of it (probably in autograph) is preserved in the Bodleian Library.

Joseph Zarco, a contemporary of Messer Leon, left two treatises. The one, entitled רב פעלים,[1] is a grammar; the other is a dictionary, and is called בעל הלשון. Manuscripts of both works are extant at the British Museum.

Moses b. Shem Ṭāb b. Ḥabīb, who about the same time emigrated from Portugal to Italy, is the author of a large grammatical work with the title פרח שושן. It is divided into six chapters. The very prolix Introduction begins with a philosophic definition of the term *Grammar*. It indulges largely in metaphysical speculations, even quoting Aristotle. In spite of its bulk the work is of hardly more than literary value, and has, like the two foregoing ones, never been published. A manuscript of it exists in the British Museum. More useful for beginners is the same author's little sketch מרפא לשון, which has been published, Venice 1546.

The literary history of Hebrew linguists properly speaking ends here. What follows is mere bibliography, and the small list appended only includes a number of names of Jewish and Christian authors. To the former group belongs Immanel b. Jequthiel, author of a grammar printed in Mantua 1557. *Menaḥem b. Judah di Lonzano* wrote a treatise in explanation of difficult words in the Talmuds,[2]

[1] Second edition, Amsterdam, 1730.

[2] See Dukes, *Litbl.*, VIII, p. 441.

styled מעריך. A large Hebrew dictionary with Latin and Italian translations was written by David de Pomis, and published Venice 1587. Moses b. Abraham Provezalis published a small compendium on grammar entitled בשם קדמון, Venice 1596. *Samuel b. Elḥanan di Archivolti* is the author of a grammar, published Venice 1602, under the title ערוגת הבשם. Finally, the famous Leon of Madena compiled a brief sketch of grammar and a vocabulary of difficult words in a work styled גלות יהודה.

Of Christian authors two names might be added to those mentioned above, viz. Conrad Pelham, who published a small but unimportant grammatical manual (1500), and Johann Boschenstein, author of a similar work, Wittenberg, 1518.

APPENDICES

I

MS. Brit. Mus. Or. 2400, fol. 62 v°.

יגאבן נדכר אלפאט גויצא עברתה פי הדא אלספר

ונורי אשתקאקהא ותצריפהא פי אלדקדוק ליקף עליהא אלמתעלם אן שא אללה תע הנני שך את דרכך ישתק מן הסר מסֻכתן ואלאמר מנה שך מתל שָׁב קוּם קָם: אתנה המה תפסירהא מתל תפסיר אתנן ואלנון אלאול גיהרי ואלנון אלאכיר מרכב ואמא אתנה פאלהֵא פיה מרכבה ותעד נזמה פאלאמר מנה עדה והו נאקץ הֵא מתל ותעל ותעש: מפתיה אליוד פיה זאיד ואכרה לי יגוז אן יכין אמרה נכר מתל נצר ואצרך ויגוז אן יכון אמרה הכר חטף מן חית אנה חסר ולו כאן ואכירה כאן יכון אמרה הכיר ביוד והדא נטיר ותחילנה אלדי אמרה החל הסר מתל ואכרה: ודמיתי אמך אלאמר מנה דְמֵה (*sic*) והדה אללפטה אעני דְמֵה להא תפסירין אלואחד ישבה מתל סֹב דְמֵה לך ואלאכר סכות מתל ודמיתי אמך: אהבו הֵבוּ אמרה הבה יחיד הבו אמרה רבים מתל זרו את יהודה: צרר רוח להדה אללגה תפסירין ציק וצר ועברתהא צר מתל צרורות בשמלותם ואמרה צרור מתל שְׁמֹר שָׁמַר: ירצחו שכמה אלהא פיה זאיד והו שכם ותצריפה שכמי שכמו מתל אם לא על שכמי אשאנה משכמו ומעלה: שערוריה אליוד פיה זאיד הומיה בוכיה ואנמא הו שערורה: בעֵרָה מֵאֹפֶה אלהֵא פיה זאידה לאן אלוקף עלי אלעין ולו כאן בערה כאן יכון מוֻנת פלדלך פסרתה משתעל ולם אפסרה משתעלה: הֵחֵלו (so) שרים אלאמר מנה הַחֲלֵה פלדלך פסרתה אמרצו ולם אפסרה מרצו ויריד בה אמרצו אלרוסא ללמלך: איסירם תפסירה אודבהם ואמרה הַיְסֵר מתל השמר יגי מנה אשמידם: יתגוררו יתגאורו מתל הגם אל האלמנה אשר אני מתגורר עמה

ואמרה התגורר: ישובו לא על תפסירה עאלי מתל הֻקַם עָל וקיל אנה
מרפוע והן אסם ישתק והועיל לא יועילו: גפן בוקק הו אמר פי גירה מתל
הנה יוה בוקק הארץ ולדלך פסרתה בורה אלעדו ולם אפסרה ביר חלק
לבם הו אמר פי גירה מתל אשר חלק יוי אלהיך אתם ולדלך פסרתה
קסמהם קלבהם ולם אפסרה אנקסם קלבהם: יערף מזבחותם הדה אללגה
להא הפסירין אלואחד מתל יערף כמטר לקחי יערפו טל ואקפא מתל
וערפו שם את העגלה וערפתו: שכן שמרון הו אסם סמוך ואלמֻכרת שָׁכֵן
מתל זְקַן זָקֵן ולה תפסירין אחדהמא גאר מתל על כל שכני הרעים ואלתאני
יפסר סאכן מתל שָׁכֵן ולאכן שכן הו אסם מן אמר ושֹׁכֵן הו אסם לא מן
אמר מתל אהב: בשנה אפרים יקח פסרוה כזי ואלנון פיה זאיד מתל
שבענה בנים ויגוז אנה אסם בראסה: נדמה שמרון יגוז אן יפסר מנבכם ויגוז
אן יפסר משבה והו אסם דכר ואסם אלמונת מנה נִדְמֶה ואמרה הָדְמֵה (*sic*)
ועבר אלמונת נדמתה: כקצף על פני מים פסרוה מתל אלזבד מן מוצעה
ולים לה אשתקאק עונותם יחידה עונה והו אסם ללמעניה וללמעניה תלאת
אסמא פי אלעבראני מַעֲנָה מתל כבחצי מענה מענית מתל קו למעניתם
ועונה מתל הדא: אהבתי לדוש אליוד זאיד ותפסירה מחבה כנתי וקיל
מחבתי ויכון אליוד פי מוצעה נדמה נִדְמָה מצדר מתל נכסף נכספת:
תרגלתי אלאמר מנה תרגל ועברה תרגל: קָחָם הו אסם הפסירה אכדהם
יליסהו עבר: לחיהם תפסירה טראותהם מתל עץ לח ולו כאן תפסירה
כדיהם לכאן לֶחְיֵיהֶם: ואט אמרה הטה מתל ואך אותך אמרה הכֵּה
והו נאקץ הֵא: אוביל אמרה הוביל: אלות שוא תפסירה חרג אסם רבים
ויחידה אלה מתל שנה שנות: כרית ברית הו מצדר ואמרה כְּרֹת מתל
שָׁמוֹר שָׁמוֹר: וחלה חרב אמרה חל מתל ושבה לאתננה אמרה שוב:
ועמי תלואים אמרה תלה מתל קרא קרואים ואלתו פיה גוהריה ולדלך
עברתה מעלקין ולם אעברה עגזין: נחומי הו אסם יחידה נחום מתל בכור:
תלאובות הו אסם רבים ויחידה תלאובה והי פרדיה פי אלמקרא: קטבך

הו מן אסם קטב סגור לבם יחתמל אנה אסם ללשחם אלדי עלי אלקלב ויחתמל אנה מצדר ויפסר אגלאק קלבהם: במשבר בנים אסם מתל כי באו בנים עד משבר: אהי דברך יחידה דֶבֶר מתל קבר קבריך: יפריא אמרה הַמְרֵה מתל במרום תמריא אמרה המרה יפליא ימצי אן כל הדה או אמרהא באָלֶף ולהדא אצל אכר יכון אמרה בהֵא

בריך יוי לעולם אמן ואמן

II

T—S. 49.

אם תעמל עלי הדה אלאשכאץ מתל מא פי אלמדכר לוגב משארכה אלמונת ללמדכר פי בקיה אלתצאריף לאגל אלאשתראך פי בעצהא עלי גהה אלחקיקה ואן לא תקף כטאב אלמונת עלי בעץ דון אלבעץ מע לזום אלחקיקה להא פי בעצהא פאן וקפת עלי בעץ אלכלם דון אלבעץ אלדי יתעדי אליה אלחקאיק לו כאן מגאזא למא זאד אכתר מן דלך ופי דלך . . . חקיקה אלכלם . . . פי . . . . . . אן יקאל כי יהיה נערות יות ? נערה ופי אלאמר היה תאמרהא היה ואלגמאעה מנהן היו ואלי בקיה אלתצריף מן עבר ועתיד אלגייר דלך לאסתחאלה תכציץ אלחקאיק ואיצא לו כאן בקולה תעלי כי יהיה נערה אלי גיר דלך ואקעה עלי גהה אלחקיקה ואסתעמאל לגה כדלך למא אסתחאל וקועהא כדלך עלי בת ואשה חתי יקאל כי יהיה בת כי יהיה אשה כמא יקאל כי יהיה נער אלא תרי למא קאל וכי יהיה איש גאז וכי יהיה נער וכי יהיה בן אלי גיר דלך למא כאן דלך חקיקה אסתעמאלהא פי אלזכרים פלים בעץ זכרים אולי מן בעץ ולא בעץ אלתצריף מן דלך בתעלם אלוחי מן בעץ למא בינת רפע אלאכתצאץ פי אלחקאיק פלמא צח דלך עלי מא בינת ועלם אסתחאלה תעלק הדה אלאלפאט בסוא מא תעלקת בהא מן אלאשכאץ וגיר תעדיהא מן וגהין אלמכצוצין דליל עלי אנהא מגאז או שרעי ליסת באלחקיקה ואמא קולה והיה היא רוכבת על החמור ליס מן הדה אלטריק בשי . . . לצחה אלאקסאם פיה וימכן עלי אקרב אלטריק למא כאן קולנה היא

מא תנתקל ותאי̈ד והיתה י[ה]יה בל תכון והיתה כמא כאן פי לגה̈ אלערב כ̇דלך פי לגה̈ [1][אלע]בראניין לאנה קד תרג̇ם פתציר . . . פילזמה מן ד̇לך וג̇היין אלד̇ין ד̇כרתהמא אמא כאד̇בי ? ואמא מבתדי מן נפסה עלי מא בי̇נת פאן קיל מנין לפט̇ה והיה תכ̇לף ללפט̇ה והיתה ומא אנכרת אג̇אזה̈ אלעבראנין (so) אללפט̇תין עלי אלתאנית̇ כמא ד̇כר צאחב אלתפסיר קיל לה מחאל אג̇אזה̈ אלעבראניין אללפט̇תין עלי ג̇הה̈ ואחדה̈ אלא אן תכון אחדהמא מג̇אז ואלאכ̇ר אלי גיר ד̇לך חקיקה̈ ואמא אן תכון ג̇מיעא חקיקתין פמחאל ביאן ד̇לך מעלום אן אללגאת עלי צ̇רבין צ̇רב לא יפרק אהלהא בין אלמד̇כ̇ר ואלמו̇נ̇ת̇ פי ציגה̈ אלאפעאל כמא יפרק בין בע̇ץ̇ אלאסמא פי אלתאנית̇ ואלתד̇כיר וצ̇רב אכ̇ר יפרק בתעליק תצריף אלאפעאל עלי אלאסמא ומא ישתק̇ מנהא ויג̇ריהא מג̇רי תכ̇ציץ אלאסמא פימא יכ̇תץ̇ בהא מן אג̇ראיהא פי אלתאנית̇ ואלתד̇כיר לאן אתבעו פי תסמיה̈ . . . . . .[1] בעצ̇הא עלאמה̈ ותליה אלתי לזמת מוצועאתהא ופיהא אלתאת̇יראת ופיהא מא אג̇אזו אחדהמא מן דון אלאכ̇ר אצטלאח מנהם ופיהא מא אג̇אזו כלי אלוג̇הין בתעלק אלאפעאל עליהא מן תאנית̇ ותד̇כיר מע מא כאן ימכן עלי בע̇ץ̇ אלוג̇וה אלתי תסמא באלתד̇כיר או תסמא באלתאנית̇ ועכסהא אלי גיר ד̇לך מן קבל אלאצטלאח אל ראי מן יקול ד̇לך ואמא אן יכונא ג̇מיעא יסמא באלאסמא אלתי תכ̇תץ̇ אלמד̇כ̇ר ובאלאסמא אלתי תכ̇תץ̇ אלמונ̇ת̇ וכד̇לך באלאפעאל אלתי תכ̇תץ̇ בהמא מע תפרקתהמא באלתאנית̇ ואלתד̇כיר ותפרקה̈ אפעאל אלמתעלק בהמא פמחאל ואד̇א כאן אלאמר כד̇לך וג̇ב לזום מא וצ̇ע פי אללגה̈ מן חקאיק אלעבאראת ומג̇אזהא למסמיאתהא עלי וג̇ה אלתי יסמא בהא מן תאנית̇הא ותד̇כירהא אלי גיר ד̇לך מן אקסאמהא וכ̇אצ̇ה̈ אל

אלחקאיק לאג̇ל אנהא מטאבקה ללמעאניהא ולא כ̇לאף פי ד̇לך
פי שי מן אללגאת מע חקאיקהא פי באב אלמטאבקה̈
ומואפקתהא למעאניהא אלא . . ? לא כ̇לאף פי אלמעני ענד אל[2]
עקלא פוג̇ב אצול אלמואפקה̈ פי אללגאת מא ואפק אלמעאני ולא
יכון בינהמא כ̇לאף פי ד̇לך אלא באן יכון אחדהמא ערבי ואלאכ̇ר
עבראני פאד̇א ראינא תגיר ען נט̇אם אלמטאבקה̈
וג̇ב אן ינט̇ר פיה וד̇לך עלי צ̇רב צ̇רב ילזם אלתגי̈ר
לנפס לגה̈ ואחדה̈ לא יתעד̇י מנהא אלי גירהא מן
אללגאת לעדם אסתעמאל הד̇ה אלעבאראת[1] בתגירה

[1] Erasure. [2] Erasure here, nothing discernible.

פיהא וללזום אלתגיר ללעבארה דון אל מעאני מ ? ודלך מתׄל כבש כשב שמלה ושלמה מלתעות מתלעות רצוא ושוב ההלכוא פ . . ? בזד ? אלי גיר דׄלך ממא לא יגׄוז אן יקאס עליהא ולא עלי מא שארכהא פי וגׄה אלתגׄיׄר לא מן אסמא ולא מן אפעאל ולא מן חרוף בל וגׄב לזומהא פי מוצׄעהא ולא יבדל פי גירהא באן יגׄעל[1] באב אלתגיר אלא וקד ראית לבעץ מן אלעלמא ומן אלמתׄאיב איצׄא באכׄראגׄ ודלך אלי חית אלמגׄאז פוגׄב אן ידאעא אלנאקל ענד נקלהא מא אסת?ד[2] מנהא ופהם פי לגה אלעבראניה ינקל דׄלך מן גיר זיאדה ונקצאן אלי אגׄלה אראד אלנאקל נקלהא לפט בלפט בשרט אן ידכר אנהא פי לגה אלעבראניה מתגירה מן גׄמלה אמתׄאלהא תגיר אלחרוף לא גיר ממא קד דׄכר אקסאמהא תגיר וצׄרב אכׄר מן תגׄיׄר

לצחה קבול דׄלך פי זְכָרִים ואסתחאלתה פי לשון נקבה אלא תרי למא קאל וכי יהיה איש יצח אן נגמד אלצׄמיר ונקול יהיו אנשים בלזום חרף אליא מן גיר תגיר אן ידכׄל פיתא ענד[3] באכׄבאר ען גאיבין פלו כאן אליא לאזמה ללגׄתין למא צח אלתגיר פיהא ענד אלגׄמע פי לגׄתין ואדׄא אעתברת הׄדׄה אללגה תגׄד אלתפרקה בין אלתאניתׄ ואלתדׄכיר מן אבאדי או אמרהא אלי כמאלהא אלי תרי במא תאמר ללמדׄכר מן הדׄה אללגה והו הַיֵה בׄקׄ הַיֵה אתה לעם ולרבים היו נכונ[ים]

[1] Marg. כבש ענד אלחכאית ומא אכׄרגׄת דׄלך פי כשב כבש ענד אלחכאיה.
[2] Hole here.
[3] Complete erasure here.

ולמסתקבל יהיה ולרבים יהיו[1]
וללמו̇נת̇ מן ד̇לך היי כ̇ך (אחותינו)
אחותינו את היי וללמסתקבל תהיה
ולרבים תהיינה כד̇לך אלתמם קאים
פיהא אלי כמאלהא עלי וג̇ה יסתחיל אן יקאל
ותהי איש כמא יקאל ותהי אשה אלי גיר
ד̇לך מן אלתצריף אלד̇י יתעלק באלמונת̇ מן לזום
ד̇לך להא פקד ת̇בת צחה̈ תעלק תצריף אל
מכ̇צוץ מן לשון היות באלמד̇כר עלי וג̇ה
יסתחיל תעלקהא באלמונת̇ עלי ג̇הה̈ אלחקיקה̈
ואלוג̇ה אלד̇י לאג̇לה ת̇בת ד̇לך פי
אלמד̇כר ליס אלא כונה חקיקה̈
פיה מת̇ל סאיר אלחקאיק אלתי לא
תכ̇רג̇ מן קצ̇איאהא פלו כאן קו̇ תעאלי
כי יהיה נער והיה הנער והיה
עלי אלי גיר ד̇לך חקיקה̈ פי

III

Zalmān Naqdān. Cod. Brit. Mus. Or. 853.

תרתי אני בלבי לדרוש ולתור בחכמת המקרא דבר כי ועד עתה גדלתי באהלי הנוקדים ובחבורת התלמידים וכאשר עבדתי עבדתי ליודעי דת שרי המקרא ותופשי התורה ותמיד רדפתי מן קורא לקורא כאשר בהרים ירדוף הקורא והרבתי להגות בספרים ישרים מובהקים מדויקים ומכל מלמדו השכלתי עד אשר יגלו לי ונודעו לי קצת שערי המקרא ומבואיה ומעגלי מישריה ויהי מדי התבונני בדברים בא לי קנאה וקנאתי בקוראי ספרי המקרא אשר עברו נתיבותיה וחלכו חקותיה והוסיפו וגרעו אותיות ותבות וישכנו עליונים למטה ותחתונים למעלה ואת הנגינות הגו מן המסלה מחוברים הפרידו מפוזרים הצמידו ורוב הפשעה זה תלוי על קצת הנוקדים המזידים אשר בזדון מהרו וברצונם עקרו ספרי ישראל ונתיב השכל המירו ועיני עברים עורו הורו והונו מלב דברי שקר עד אין חקר הספרים לעקר ולהכשיל רבים בתורה וימאנו לעמול להשבית עמלם עד השקיפם בספרים טובים

[1] Erased.

הנאהבים על כן פטרו עצמם מן הראיה ועשו ברמיה את רוב מלאכתם בהשענם על בינתם התעו רבים בפשלתם בשקריהם ובפחזותם זקנים שגו בנקודתם בחורם מנגינתם כי עברו על אמונתם ועל ספרים קבלו משכורתם למען השחיתם וכ . . . הם כי שקר עשו וחתו ובשו ונוקשו במפעלם לי ידעו מימינם ומשמאלם . . . וכו׳

The Introduction ends:

שלמו דברי ר׳ זלמן ומלוצותיו וחרוזותיו ויסד ספר זה של דקדוק הנקרא עין הקורא ושמו יקותיאל בר יצחק הכהן זלה״ה

זה הספר עין הקורא המאור את עיני קוראיו
לנתיב דעת זו עין מורה כי טוב רב מצא כל מוצאיו
משכיל שכלו משוש יפרה הן עליו יגילו ראיו
אוהבי יודו את הבורא׳ נותן מפיו בין ליראיו

IV

Solomon b. Abba Māri Jarḥai. Cod. Montefiore.

אמר שלמה בן אבא מרי ירחיי ימי פקדה ולילי עמל הנחלתי וירחי שוא בהפקד מאור עיני אשר אמרתו להשאיר ברכת ידיעת הלשון העברי על ידי יצאתי מרעה אל רעה כאיש נתעה אל יאמין בשוא וראיתי תוחלתי כי נכזבה ועני ישראל בלשון מאד מורה אין קורא בצדק ואין מחזיק באמונת הדבור אם להתעסקות בחכמות גדולות והיות חכמת הדקדוק נקלה אם לליאות אם לחסרון הלמוד כי אין מורה וכל הרוצה ליטול את השם שם עצם במקרה ומקרה כעצם יטול את פעל ה׳ בלשון הברואה ומלתו על לשון בני אדם לא יביטו ידיעת הקלים והכבדים עליהם לטרח ולאו נשוא בנושא משא כבד ונטל החול יטול אמרתי לחבר הספר הזה הקטן ואולי לקצורו ידרשו גוים אליו בנה בניתי בית זבול לו נכון על אלמיו ואליו נשען על שני העמודים האחד בידיעת הדקדוק והשני בביאור הפעלים והשמות ומלות הטעם למלאות חפץ ומחשבות חרוץ ועם זה כנף זאת החכמה נחפה בכוסף (*sic*) הקריאה ואברותיה בירקרק חרוץ כלל הדקדוק בו לפי מערכת הקדומים נעדר ופירוש הפעלים על מקומו יבא איש לא נעדר

בית הוד שפת עבר להקימו אני אבנה בענייו לו שני עמודים
דקדוק ובאור סוד פעליה בתוך ספר קראתיהו לשון למודים